# Word Fest, Celebrating our Journeys

## Mississauga Writers Group

# Word Fest, Celebrating our Journeys

Layout and Formatting Copyright © 2015 Mississauga Writers Group
Cover Design Copyright © 2015 Shutterstock, Inc.
Individual Pieces in this Collection © 2015 Individual Authors
Book Editing by Elizabeth Banfalvi
Copy Editing by Veronica Lerner

First published in Mississauga in 2015 by Mississauga Writers Group

\*\*\*

ISBN-13: 978-1517053338

ISBN-10: 1517053331

Mississauga Writers Group,
Mississauga, Ontario, Canada

http://www.mississaugawritersgroup.com/

http://www.facebook.com/MississaugaWritersGroup

All enquiries: info@mississaugawritersgroup.com

# In Appreciation

Mississauga Writers Group officially began in January 2013. Since then, we have published our first anthology in 2014, and now we are proud to present our second anthology. We have some wonderful new writers and poets, and happily our regular writers have also contributed. Enjoy our new anthology and the originality of our writers.

*Elizabeth Banfalvi*

# Contributing Writers

Elizabeth Banfalvi

Scott Berger

Meena Chopra

Angela Ford

Mark David Garden

Marijana Gmitrovic

John Henderson

Kim MacMurray

Hamzah Moin

Joseph A. Monachino

Milena Munteanu

Daniela Oana

Jasmine Sawant

G. Ian Stout

Hans V. von Maltzahn

# Table of Contents

# Our Fable of Authors

*by Elizabeth Banfalvi*

Once upon a time, in a Fest of Book, three people met. Ian, Samna and Elizabeth were their names. Ian spread the word of the "author" and the others attended to his words. The afternoon went pleasantly well as Ian wove the tale of "author" and the ways thereof. He spoke of the other worldly pursuits of groups, workshops and gatherings. Elizabeth listened and pondered. She finally spoke to the other two of a tale of beginnings as a group in the village of Mississauga. The other two became excited and a plot was devised to start a round table of like souls.

Samna, being a purveyor of wisdom in technology, began to weave her magic. She reached out to the fortress of the library and received permission to summon others from the Fest to the new gathering.

The summons was answered by many faraway villages such as Streetsville, Port Credit, Meadowvale, the borough of Scar, and so on. Many would come at the beginning of 2013 AD but where would the assembly be held? One of the brave Ladies of the Order named Jasmine offered her fortress and would be the host to the many.

Our quest of the round table started. Knights and Ladies came – some well versed and some not as much. Some were of a poetic way while others wrote of times passed and murderous pursuits.

An agenda was prepared and read at the first coming together. Most were puzzled but accepted it as a tribute to the highest. Nicholas came so did Bev and Rashmi. Rashmi, though quiet and contemplative, joined in the speakings and wrote great words of the gathering.

An appellation was decided and Samna's wisdom of technology was again honed and a website was partaken. Time journeyed on and Ian came and went on his worldly pursuits.

---

Eventually a scripture was born of the writings of the members and "Word Fest" was its name. The members journeyed to many other villages and met other partisans.

More pursuits came to the group of many. Many came and gave offerings and were read and perused. Many went on and had writings of the "author" and journeyed their own route. Many stayed and formed a strong and unified table. All hold their mighty pens high and look upwards knowing their crusade has only begun.

Angela – The Princess in the Tower
Daniela – The Princess of the Petites
Elizabeth – The Queen of the Healing Soul
Hamzah – The Court Jester
Hans – The Guard of the Internet
Ian – Lancelot of the Traveling Pants
Jasmine - Our Lady who weaves Silken Tales
John – The Knight of the Forbidden Lust
Joseph – The Time Traveler
Kim – The Shaman of Psychic Arts
Marijana – The Lady Seeking Wisdom of the Pen
Mark – The Quiet Knight
Meena –Lady of the Poetic Prowess
Milena – Princess of Quiet Pursuits
Scott – The Knight who Came From Afar

# *Angela*

## Angela's Story

*When do you find the time to write?*

I have been asked this question many times in interviews. My answer, "I don't". Then there is that pause and I notice the same expression. So I elaborate. "I write. And try to find time to fit everything else in". Just ask my family. They will tell you all the strange times of the day and places I write. I am never without a device I can write on; whether it is my laptop, phone or even the old fashion pen and paper. But there is one place I am not allowed to write—the dinner table. I have been frisked! Normally this would be mom's rule but not in my house. My teenager lays down the law. I am very lucky to have a supportive, understanding and loving family. With a great sense of humor!

Recently asked if I always wanted to be a writer, took my thoughts back to my childhood memories. Born and raised in Nova Scotia, Canada's Ocean Playground, in a family of nine; my Mom and Dad and six siblings. Yes, a very busy household! I am number six in the mix. My oldest sister's friend coached Highland Dancing and I joined when I was four. For the next eleven years this became my every other breath. At eleven I made the cut for the Scotia Highland Dancers; a group of forty dancers from across the province who performed at various functions. In 1979 Nova Scotia began an annual tradition known as the International Tattoo. The Scotia Highland Dancers were invited. Being the youngest of eight hundred participants awarded me with a formal introduction to the Queen Mother who had been visiting the province and attending the event. Honored to have met her will remain in my heart forever. When a knee injury prevented my love of dancing competitively and for pleasure, I found myself enthralled in reading. As a teenager I babysat for my sister and discovered her romance novels. From then I have never been without a book and found myself dreaming to write one.

*Did I know then I wanted to be a writer?*

The question had been asked so many times I decided to sort through a box of things I kept close to my heart from my childhood. I found my grade school journal. My mom kept it as all moms do. I do the same. I flipped through the pages and surprised myself with the last page of each grade. There that same question with empty boxes to check beside each profession. *What do you want to be when you grow up?* Ah! There on every page of every grade -- my answer! I had mostly all boxes checked off. If anyone had looked at this journal, they'd think I had no idea what I wanted to be when I grew up. I did. Just by scanning the pages and seeing the many check marks. I didn't want to be all those professions. I simply wanted to write about all those professions in the many stories in my heart—in my mind. Never tell someone you hear voices in your head without further explanation that you are a writer. I wanted to write but it just wasn't the right time of my life to do so.

I left Nova Scotia in the early nineties to venture out west to the Rockies in Alberta with my fiancé. Both of us had worked for Westray Coal; the coal mine that sadly took the lives of twenty-six coal miners. After our son was born with a dislocated hip, we ventured further to British Columbia to be close to Sick Kids Hospital. Our son's first year in a body cast to correct the dislocation kept us busy. It has also kept him out of a wheel chair. He is now twenty-two. Our daughter was born five years later on Vancouver Island where we spent another five years before the move to Ontario where we presently reside. It was after my daughter's birth that I picked up a journal again and began to write. My favorite place to write is the beach. There is something about the water and sunsets that inspire me. A move to Ontario left me as a single parent raising two kids with two jobs. My journal went back in the box for some time. As my kids grew into young adults, so did my time to write. I have always returned to the written word; a passion that lives within me, whether it is to read or to write. Finally my time to write had come.

In 2013 after many query letters I was offered my first contract with Books to Go Now; a small traditional publisher out of Seattle. Though I must share I wasn't sure if it was real. I had so many refusals but what made me wonder -- the offer came on April 1st. Yes, April fool's Day. Two days later I heard from the publisher again if I had received the offer. I then performed the 'Happy Dance'.

My first book *Closure* was published in 2013. The idea sparked from the many years volunteering in my kids' school. A parent helper, lunchroom supervisor and school council chair awarded me with an Award of Distinction in public education. Our school council hosted cyber safety seminars with our local police to educate parents to keep our kids safe online. My book, *Closure*, is about an FBI team who track online predators lurking teens. I believe my plotting came from a combination of being a protective mom and inspiring writer.

It has been a long road. It hasn't always been easy but it has been rewarding. There are many long devoted hours to writing, editing and promoting; besides fitting everything else in to the day. Some days I wish for a thirty-six hour day. Then again I would probably spend those hours with my kids or writing. A writer seldom sleeps. Then there is the day job. Yes, I work full time. Eight hours of my day, Monday through Friday are spent with a great team in Finance at the School Board head office. Numbers by day, words by night.

Life brings us joy and sorrow. It brings hardship and heartache. And sometimes life just happens. I'm a mom first; always have been, always will be. But now they help Mom. They taught me how to interact on social media. Though they probably regret it some days as I always seem to have some sort of device in my hands. But at least I abide to the dinner table rule they enforce. They also help along my journey with assistance at an author signing event and creating promotional materials. I am blessed with amazing talented children. Not only have my children inspired me, my parents are my inspiration to write happily-ever-after. Whether it is a romantic suspense or a sweet or spicy contemporary, I love my HEAs. My second book published Unforgettable Kiss is dedicated to my parents of sixty years and counting. They are my real-life fairy tale. After divorce and raising kids on my own; they not only give me strength to keep moving forward but they give me hope within that true love does exist.

After publishing suspense with a dash of romance and a spicy romance with a dash of suspense, I published *Closure*'s sequel *Forbidden*. In 2015, I will release the third in the series called Obsessed. In between I have published another romantic suspense called *Surrender* and a few sweet contemporaries and Christmas romances. I love anthologies and collaborating with other authors both from my publisher and with my writers group.

# Closure

Chapter One

Jessica Resario held her finger firmly on the trigger and waited in the dark, listening to the echo of footsteps on the stairs.

"Remain focused Agent Resario," she reminded herself.

When the bedroom door flew open, she sucked in her breath.

A dark figure appeared. He wore a balaclava, so the only part of his face she could see was his eyes, but she could tell by the surprised look in them that he didn't expect to see her. "Jessica!" he exclaimed.

She needed to remain professional, although she wanted to ask him how the hell he knew her.

He gave her a cocky smile and lunged forward. She went down hard. The gun flew across the room. She jumped up and ran to the top of the staircase. Only inches behind her, he grabbed her arm. His fingers twisted so powerfully she felt a fierce burn on her skin. With only seconds to act, fear-driven strength crafted the thrust of her raised knee. She stunned him long enough to shake free of his hold and sprint down the stairs. She reached for the front door and swung it hard enough to make it slam against the wall. She hoped the loud bang and the open door would lead him outside. She ran into the living room.

He reached the bottom of the stairs with only the open door in sight. She breathed in relief; the open door led him outside into the darkened night. Cramped in a tight area behind the sofa, she gently pulled the heavy drapes back just a small crack and peered over the window ledge. She could see nothing but the shadows of tall trees and beyond, an empty street. No sign of a person. Not even a dog barked.

*Is this how my life will end—alone?* She wondered.

Suddenly reality hit her. She let no one in. Brave at work, yet in her personal life, she didn't have the courage to confess her true feelings to Tom. The murder of her parents ten years before kept her from loving, for fear of losing again. All she had was her work, and her work put her life into the hands of a serial killer.

*Is he gone*? She wondered.

Jess crawled a little farther around the sofa, her knees trembling. She moved slowly, listening for a footstep or a breath taken; she needed a better look. Gently pulling herself up and the heavy drapes open,   she peered with one eye over the window ledge. It looked as dark outside as it did inside.

*Who is he?* She wondered. How did he know her?

*Is it safe to leave?* She knew she had to get out of there.

Her legs cramped, and she shifted her weight, and then stifled a cry of pain. She'd lost her footing when she fled and missed the last couple of steps. Shaking in fear, she felt pain in her leg. Jess fought for air.

*Where is he?* Her eyes tried to focus in the darkened house.

The front door was still open, about ten feet away. She rose again to have a better look around the drapes, but nothing could be seen except dark shadows and a quiet, dimly-lit street. She stood up slowly from that tiny area, and adjusted to the darkness, then limped to the front door with her hand holding tightly to her bad leg. Her purse was still where she'd left it on the deacon's bench in the front hall. Her car was still parked in the driveway. She walked out but didn't close the door. Jess nervously scouted the outside area for him, and clutched her purse in one hand as the other dug inside it for her keys.

She unlocked the car door, slipped in, then, with trembling hands, she keyed the ignition. For the first time, she could relax.

Clearing the driveway at last, she asked for "home." The car's device dialed the number. Home for Agent Resario was her boss, Tom.

"Jesus Jess, I was worried!" Tom's anxious voice came over the speaker.

"I'm still breathing," she answered as she tried to remain the strong, independent woman she portrayed to her team. She held tightly onto the steering wheel to keep her hands from shaking. This time someone got under her skin. She'd not yet learned to follow the protocol. She did things her way instead of the Bureau's way. She had taken another long shot, and "followed her gut instinct," as she called it. It was fortunate for young Rebecca Smythe though. Jess saved the girl from becoming victim number four.

"At least you're still breathing." His tone seemed genuine. She knew it was more than that. She'd felt it for a long time. To Jess, to the team, to the world, he remained silent. He appeared solid, professional and almost cold-hearted—or so he thought. She remained silent as always, in denial of his love and her own. She realized she'd let her thoughts wander and switched her focus back to the case.

"My hunch was right. He went for her and got me. She and her parents cleared out before he arrived. They're safe. It was dark, he was in black and a balaclava, but I think he recognized me. He called me by my first name."

"I want you to take cover for a day or so. You know where to go?" Tom said.

**** 

He didn't say much, but it was enough for Jess to understand. All he heard was the dial tone so Tom Erickson turned to his colleagues.

"She's alive. It was too dark for her to get a visual of him during a struggle. She's on her way to the safety point. But he knew her. He called her Jessica."

"It's been a long night. Go home and get some sleep. We'll begin again tomorrow once we know Jess is safe." Tom dismissed the team and made one last call to the local authorities to process the scene Jess had just left. Tom grabbed his jacket off the back of his chair and turned out the lights.

\*\*\*\*

Jess arrived at the airport. She had no one to talk to about what she'd just survived. She didn't have any friends, except for the team. She respected Tom's direction to go to the safety point. She just wished he was with her. She needed to talk to someone.

At 41, Tom was the head of internet security for the FBI in the San Francisco office. Tom physically fit the description of tall, dark and handsome. Something mysterious and dark about him made him very intriguing. His expression was always the same, always serious. She would need to search long to remember if she'd ever seen him smile at anyone. He always dressed in a black suit and tie. But Tom was different with Jess; he smiled when they were alone. He lightened up and joked with her. Most important, he listened to her when she needed to talk and right now she needed him.

Jess closed her eyes, and took a deep breath as the plane began its take-off. She didn't notice anyone else on the plane—not even the attendants. She slept through the whole flight and did not wake until the plane landed. As she walked through the terminal, she felt empty. She'd taken nothing with her but her purse. She'd left everything at the other end of the country— even her dignity. Outside the airport, she hailed a cab.

Memories suddenly filled her mind as they drove past a park by the ocean, and she remembered playing there as a child. Jess loved the ocean. It gave her a sense of peace and serenity. The salt air, the sound of the waves crashing against the rocks, and the way the sun shone across the ripples and sparkled, seemed magical. While most little girls dreamed of fairy tales and Prince Charming, Jess dreamed of the beach, the ocean, and the warm breeze. Seeing that park beside the ocean overwhelmed her with both happiness and emptiness. The memories of good times only reminded her that her parents would no longer be at the summer home when she arrived. The cab stopped and Jess returned from her memories to the present and paid the driver.

Jess read the sign above the store, *The Village Boutique*. She smiled, remembering the first time her mother brought her there. They were shopping for a "tea dress" as her mother called it. It became an annual event, along with tea at "high noon" at the *Village Tea House*. Tears welled up in her eyes but her heart smiled remembering those treasured moments with her mom. Jess took a deep breath as she placed her hand on the big brass door handle of The Village Boutique.

Inside it felt the same, and smelled the same. Not a single thing had changed from what she remembered. A familiar voice came from inside the store,

"Jessica Resario, is that you?"

A woman with white hair walked toward her and there was something about her that looked familiar and heart-warming.

"My God, it *is* you! You've grown into such a beautiful woman. You look just like your mother."

Before Jess knew it, the woman had locked her arms around her in a hug. Jess smiled politely at Mrs. Walker.

"Hi, Mrs. Walker, thank you for the compliment."

"Oh, you were such a doll when you were little. It's nice to see your manners are still with you. Your mother brought you up right."

Jess just smiled as she remembered how amazingly fast the woman could speak.

"I was so sorry to hear about your parents, Jessica. It was just so terrible. We all wondered if you would ever come back to us. The house has sat empty for so long now. Are you planning to stay for a while?"

Jess nodded. She had become a woman of few smiles and less words. It was just very hard for her to get close to another human being since that awful night. How ironic that her first day at college, which should have been the beginning of her future, was the last day of her family.

Mrs. Walker continued rambling about the community, interrupting herself now and then to holler out, and "Sandra! Sandra! "

Another familiar voice came from behind her.

"Oh my God, it's Jess!" Jess knew the voice and smiled with delight. "Sandra Walker," she said. The two women hugged.

Sandra smiled and flashed her left hand in Jess's face. "Well, actually, its Sandra Cameron now."

"You married Billy Cameron after all."

"Well, he goes by Bill now, but yes, the one and only guy in my heart."

Mrs. Walker continued to ramble and both girls laughed as they always did. Sandra's mom was well-known for her fast tongue, and referred to by many as the village know-it-all. It was good to see some familiar faces, but too much when Sandra invited her for dinner. What would Jess talk about besides the initial, it's-nice-to-see-you, how-have-you-been to where-have-you-been and what-have-you been-up-to? Questions Jess was just not ready to answer yet.

So she told her friend she was tired from travelling and the airlines lost her luggage, which was why she'd come to the boutique. The ladies were polite. They called a cab to take her to the one and only place she could go to—a place she hadn't been since the awful tragedy. The thought terrified her.

Distracted with thoughts of returning to the place that was once most memorable, but now horrific, Jess didn't pay much attention to the pale green old truck parked on the road at the end of the driveway. The man inside the truck made eye contact with her as the cab slowly turned in. Usually her investigative mind would have studied his face and stored it in her memory, but her mind was busy convincing herself she was ready to deal with her parents' murders.

"This is a beautiful spot," the cab driver announced.

"My mom's dream beach home," she sadly replied. Jess's memory flashed backed to when she was seven and her parents first took her to their new summer home. There was lots of excitement in her parent's car that day. It was her mother's dream beach home, and that's exactly what it had become to Jess also until that fateful night.

Her love of the ocean was passed down from mother to daughter. Jess lived on the West Coast now, to be near the ocean—the one place she could always go to when things were tough and she felt all alone. She hadn't been able to make herself go to the East Coast, to that ocean—it was too painful. Now, she had no choice; it was time to deal with the past.

"What an amazing view of the ocean. It's deceiving. You wouldn't know from the driveway as you only see the trees," the cabbie remarked.

"My mom called the property, 'the enchanted forest with the hidden secret of the ocean view,' " Jess informed him. The house's simple design was made up of two gently curved overlapped roofs. Most of the windows faced south to capture the spectacular view of the coastline, and also to optimize daylight. There was something about the type of windows used, that Jess couldn't quite recollect.

"The clerestory operable windows make the difference to allow the light to penetrate throughout the house. It should help reduce your heating bills," the cabbie said as he put the car in park.

"That's what they're called. I couldn't recollect what my mom called them. She was an environmentalist and interior designer. I guess I didn't pay much attention when I was younger, "she said and then chuckled to herself. She pictured her father's smirk when he tried to explain in simple terms, that it saved money. He could always make her laugh, even when she was sad. That was her greatest memory of him.

"Miss," the cabbie said, as he opened her door.

"Thank you, sir. You know a thing or two about windows?" she asked with a smile.

"A few," he admitted and smiled too. "I'm also a contractor for home renovations, if you ever need anything fixed up." He handed her his business card. She handed him the fare, thanked him again and retrieved her bags.

The cab slowly retreated down the driveway and she stood there for a few moments. Jess took a deep breath, and tried to persuade herself to go in. She reached for the key in her pocket as she walked up the cobblestone steps, then turned the key in the lock. The door opened and she froze. From here, she could easily see the remarkable view of the ocean. There was no need to walk through the house. "Infinite Appeal," were the words Jess recollected her mom saying the first day they looked at it with the realtor. Her mom had immediately said, "This is the one."

The rest of the house was amazing too. It had an open plan with a few interior walls and a band of clerestory windows that allowed the sunlight to penetrate deeply into the far end of the house. To her right were two steps down into her room. It still looked like the pink princess fairy-tale room her mother designed for her. Nothing had been touched. She dropped her bags on the steps of her room and continued down the entry into the "great room" as her mom had called it.

Straight ahead lay the dining room with a colossal oak dining table in the middle of the room. Many family meals were eaten there looking out at the ocean.

To the right was a massive stone fireplace that captured one entire wall. Before it, inviting armchairs and a chaise lounge stood to one side. On many nights, the family sat by the fire, talking, and reading. The window seat then caught her eye; that nook that she would crawl into as a little girl to read and some nights fall asleep listening to her parents talk. They were so in love with each other, and adored Jess. To her, they were her fairy-tale.

She'd had so much before the murders. For years she had forbidden herself to love for fear of loss but for the past several hours, it was all she could think about. Jess knew she was too hard on herself. After all, she was only human.

Lost in her thoughts, and feeling sorry for herself, she discovered her hand on the banister that led upstairs to her dad's den. Most of the second level was open. The kitchen to the left of the staircase entry consisted of stainless steel appliances and cherry wood cabinetry—the island, the cabinets and the hutch. Beyond the great room was the master suite, a place Jess desired to leave behind that closed door.

A sudden knock at the door startled her and she turned around. The door slowly opened and a voice called out her name. Jess smiled. Before she even turned, she knew who it was. "Mr.

Roberts. How are you?"

He looked the same, just older. He and his wife lived a half-mile up the road and since the Resarios only spent their summers at the beach home, Mr. Roberts agreed to be the home's caretaker during the off-season. Even after the tragedy, the agreement continued.

"I'm fine Miss Jessica. I heard through the grapevine that you were in town." Jess knew that Mrs. Walker must have called him the minute she left the boutique.

"How is Mrs. Roberts?"

"Oh, she's wonderful, as always. She wanted to come by and see you but thought it best to let you settle in first. She said to call if there was anything you need. She sent some food and necessities for you."

Mrs. Roberts, the village sweetheart always treated Jess as the daughter she never had. Jess's eyes filled with tears. There were kind people in this world just like her parents. She had forgotten that. In her area of work, she only saw and dealt with the bad ones who wanted to hurt, not help.

"She's so sweet to do that for me. I feel bad for not visiting for so long," Jess said with tears in her eyes.

"It's okay Jessica, we both understand how difficult it must be for you," Mr. Roberts replied then he excused himself to get the packages from the car.

Jess watched him go out then turned her focus to her parent's closed bedroom door, her thoughts of the night they were murdered there. Her heartbeat increased and a tear ran down her cheek as she imagined the fear her parents must have felt. She heard Mr. Roberts return and hoped he hadn't seen her tears.

"I've kept the house as it always was," Mr. Roberts told her, and

Jess understood what he meant. The home had been cleaned up and put back to the way it was prior to that awful night. She was indebted to the Roberts. They always protected her.

"Thank you."

Mr. Roberts kissed her on the cheek. "Call if you need anything else," he told her, and then left.

Jess gripped the banister with one hand; her eyes closed, and then slowly climbed the stairs. The steps curved and lead up to her dad's den.

Once inside, she saw that nothing had been touched. It was as though he was coming back to his desk. When she was a child she would sit on the guest bed in the far corner and watch him work. She loved watching him; he was always so focused. She wasn't sure what he did. All that her parents would ever say was that Dad was working. It was when she became a teenager that she asked more questions, but only learned that her Dad worked for the government. Jess accepted it—mostly because she was a teenager and absorbed in her own life. She wished she had been more involved in their lives—asked more, and listened more.

Why? Why were they taken from her?

Now having full disclosure of her Dad's job and what it entailed, she understood why it wasn't discussed. She had a great deal of respect for her father and his decision to keep that part of him distant. She wasn't even certain if her mother knew all that his job entailed.

Her fingers flipped through the Day-Timer on his desk. Her left hand reached over to touch his reading glasses. A tear ran down her cheek. Coming back here, after all these years was more strenuous than she had imagined. Selling their family home in Washington years before had been a little easier. They'd only lived in that home for a few years. It was the summer home where family memories were made.

It was close to sunset. She noticed the house beginning to darken and went back downstairs to start a fire, then realized she hadn't eaten a thing for over twenty-four hours. She still had one thing left to do before she ate—send a text message to Tom that she arrived safe.

Her message was delivered and read in an instant. "That man never stops working," she said out loud, then set her phone down on the counter. She was making a cup of tea and preparing a plate of the food Mrs. Roberts sent for her, when her phone beeped with a text message.

*Good to hear. Take care. I worry.*

Jess read the message a few times. Maybe someone *would* miss her. She just wouldn't allow it. She knew Tom respected her privacy. She also knew she had feelings for him. She just wished she had the courage to tell him.

*Thank you for reading the beginning of Closure. I hope you enjoyed it. Closure is available in eBook, Paperback and Audio at Amazon, Smashwords, Barnes & Noble and Kobo. If you pick it up or any of my books, I would love to hear from you!*

# *Daniela*

# Daniela's Story – Poetry, Unveiled

I began noticing poetry at about twelve years old. It is then that I began to take pleasure in reading sweet short poems and quotes alike. With boys suddenly in mind, I soon started writing my own longing poems. Writing remained a practiced craft I never parted from, yet one always kept to myself. Listening to soft, slow music was and remains a form of inspiration, as was my pondering nature, known to be with my "head in the clouds."

Reflecting on these early years, I now see that I embodied many of the typical characteristics of an inner poet. Being of a timid and quiet nature, I found poetry a swell form of expression. I also constantly found myself longing for young happiness found in two. I was and still am of an old-fashioned nature, delighting in traditional aspects, in classic films, often attracted to tragedy, viewed as a form of romanticism. Though social and outgoing, my interests and comfort in my introverted nature often made me feel – perhaps like many of us – well – different. Through creating poetry, however, I perceived this as a fine, unique and thus accepted characteristic. Ironically, I later began to seek being different, appreciating it as a form of art. Being artistically-inclined – paint, draw, photograph - I also attempted applying this uniqueness in my writing and artistic sense.

My poetry has always been deeply dear and important to me, more so in the recent years in which I've felt more confident as a writer. What has given me this 'boost' is also a desire to read more poetry and learn about different styles of poetry and poets, both traditional and contemporary. Getting involved with writers from either poetry slams or writer groups, have also further fired my passion. This not only places me in a different stage in life, but also in a different stage as a writer.

Over the years, I have noticed through my writing how I both matured as an individual and as a writer.

Poetry is a passion I often wonder who I would be, and what I would do, without.

# Whispering Voice

Echoing voice
Distantly heard
Past the dried trees
Over decadent soil.

Whispering voice
Creeps over my ear
Like a coiling lizard
Nesting over its concoction.

Curious voice
Draws me right in
Off my path
Into sudden darkness.

Friendly voice
Serenades my name
Through cooled breath
To breathe in and choke on.

Pleading voice
Calling me over
For a promised treat
In the soil cracks.

Impatient voice -
For time is pressing.
A slapping tail
Tapping claws.

Furious voice
Wailing in my head
Tugging at my feet
Showing its face!

Utter silence
Creeps over my ears

Like morning kisses
Muted in final flashbacks.

# Look What I Found

I know I'm the starved,
Hungry in my hiding.
My mind is that place,
As fake as this world.

I am the Poet in a best-seller
And you, its bitter-sweet words.
I was brought into this world
Now dragged on its soil.

I'm the prized, holding pride
I'm still dragged into corners
Yet still under the spotlight
All friends enjoy the sight.

I am a local in my city
But a traveler on this earth.
Who's to blame?
The answers are all the same.

With adoring, eager eyes
You lift my hands, sunken in soil.
A struggle with warmth to spur,
It is my heart that needs it most.

The Good, the Evil got me to my knees,
Lined my wrinkles, took my beauty,
Slowed my heart and sloed my eyes.

Look at you,
Brought before my knees,
I may have found a best friend
With my day-dreams coming true.

I have yet to feel this way
Since my childhood soil-free hands.
I pray, walking a new path,
Am I taking on or risking a chance?

Look what I found -
Gold in this muddy soil
Dirty among rocks
Shining underneath it all.

## Spring

You tore down the vines
The green grapes so sweetly plump
Those we'd savour in our wine
That we'd cheer to all those nights

You dried out the garden
And let weeds overtake our nest.
All your power let unleashed
Hit like thunder burning crops

Such fury your chest held
And such bitterness you lashed
While I fed you grape by grape
Water from my urn to drink

You cried at the end of it
With hands clutching your own hair
That I'd stoke so tenderly
Praising every spec of you

You were without my arms to nestle in
Or fall into, this time around.
I caught the ground you've pushed me to
Mud and worms in both my hands

You avenged your own tears
And the entity of unforeseen misery
Blaming me for rising
And start tidying our ravaged garden

But outnumbered and too week
You succumbed to your own madness
As I raised my handkerchief,
My white flag to you, poor enemy

You spun around and turned your back
To flee away and hide your face
While I waited in our devastated nest
My eyes more so than the wreck itself

You've since been lost and lone
From losing the battle and me altogether
And I've been found dead
After what's become of us and our Eden

But good fortune has emerged
Along your path, beneath my feet
For time has finally been kind
And has brought Spring back to us

You lost no battle after all
But a few tears to feed your newfound soil
And the sun has tidied the turmoil in my eyes
Feeding the sprouts in my newfound garden

# Fall

My roots deepened to keep warm
As did my love to sooth you more.
You tried sprouting in the Fall
But the frost came bite you hard
So you stood by to keep warm

Your roots cooled like the Fall
As did your heart towards mine
And like a trembling branch leaf,
Your hand let go from holding mine
So you went about your flight

You soared high over the winds
But the raindrops trampled you back down
Into my hands that I held out
But you seeped through my fingers
And hit the ground as did my knees

We found our only path beneath us
That would eventually bring Summer rays
But not before we lose our colour,
Start to wither to the Winter
And beg for soil's leftover life

But Fall's curse cannot be broken
And no leaf escapes its fate
Nor does any path evade the frost
Like that set over your heart
So we walked on the Valley of Death

# Your Poem

As pure black coal is found
So true love we found abound.
Better than onyx can awe,
In our coal, there was no flaw

As blazing coal turns hot red
So your love began to shred.
Even rubies couldn't stand
The decadence in our land

As helpless as a white dove
So you have tampered with love.
Our white-flaking charred coal
Now an undug opal's lost soul
      ***

As a wind-breaking mountain top
So our love, gusts, it could stop.
We stood just as solemnly tall
Though on earth, we were so small

As fierce lava can suddenly spur
So your love soon turned to blur.
Tempest thunder struck the sky
Lava swallowed my last cry

As hard magma's all that's left
So our love and mountain cleft
Are but a wounded remnant
Whose lifespan has spent
      ***

As the brilliance of a star
So love blinded from afar.
My prayer granted in my palm
I dedicate to Love our psalm

As marvelous as a flying comet
So you dedicate me a sonnet
Of the love you've taken back
Marvelously scribed in black

As dead meteors soon cool
So thrown stones, our land, rule -
Hurled from your hands to my feet
This poem you end with my defeat

# Elements

Lamp posts reluct in glowing their light
Down upon the dirt snowflakes melt on,
Who parachute right into the war zone
But the first hours' worth never make it
So they float nation-serving back lampwards.

Their arm-linked slushy corpse still hum
Their anthem to their marching foes
Whose boots step onto this mud of men,
No snow left of them but muddy graves,
Buried in the fibers of their flag.
                *\*\**

They worked the fronts with slush and mud
For the snowfall dashing by the lamp posts,
Snowflakes coming down greater in number,
Landing like bombs, blowing those boots,
Few, the battlefield, meant to surmount.

They join the mud men's echoing hum,
Setting foot where their corpse have led the way,
Wounded not into slush but cold-bloodedly fit
They trample boots and helmets boom by boom,
Till their snow-crystals arm-link into ice sheets.
                *\*\**

They worked the fronts with bombs by sea shores,
Breaking the ice their enemies drowned through,
Forced to sink arm-linked with rivalrous ships,
Buried in the stitches of their flag,
Saluting goodbye the lamp posts' coming army.

These floating snowflakes soar like vultures,
Dashing left and right, eye-scanning the sky.
Like a shaken snow globe filled with aircrafts,
They fire bullets, dropping bombshells
Plunging in spirals to their air-show death.

They worked the sky like beeping radars
Their dropped shells plowed enemy ground,
Buried in the sky of their flying flag,
Leaving trenches for the troops down-pouring
Past the lamp posts with tautly drawn rifles,

Multiplied as though through a fly's eye
Or as through growing, chasing fire flames,
Licking men's backs, melting like snowmen,
Others like roaches, in trench hideouts crawl,
Knowing the above enemy fire chars unforgiving.
***
They worked the fronts with ash and fire
Buried at the foot of their lowered flag.
The unvisited lamp posts have shut like a flame,
The blue sky of a newborn day announcing
A victorious snowstorm, its Fallen Flakes now a flood.

## Your Shot

I crop my life
Edge to edge
Only the best
Foregrounded,
To background
The darkness
Shading my eyes.
My face didn't make
The crop lines.

I filter my eyes
From pouring salt,
Filtering alike
The ball in my throat
That brought along
This bitter taste.
Though flavorless,
I still choke.
Ain't no filter
For this ache.

Here's my shot -
A headless gal
Holding flowers
On her chest
Burned to ashes
Like her palms
That wiped tears
Of acid salt.
Now look carefully
At the uncharred bullet
Perfectly aimed
At my chest.
That's your shot.

# Anxiety

The storm is shouting at me
While my nerves attempt to calm
Rummaging through Do's and Don'ts
To shun panic and shut shutters
But they slam, fling and flutter
Wailing, bullying leftover reason
Thus my nerves slowly give up
So I can't leave the house

It growls out hostage debris
Tiles and shingles, glass and splinters
From my house, undone to pieces
To hit hard and not think straight
While my mind attempts to settle
To gather both feet and flee off
But they're beaten by the beams
So I can't leave the house
　　　***

The bombs tremor at my feet
Or my feet do and they thump
While I've little to no time
To diffuse my growing chaos
But their ticking – loud as cymbals –
Echo painfully deep in my head.
I'm either disoriented or blown.
So I can't hear what you're saying

They blast – finally within me –
While my chest attempts to quiet
To take in full breaths again
To see through thick blur again
But the blow took all my air,
The bomb's and my time elapsed.
There was no red wire to cut.
Still can't hear what you're saying

# The Mentor

You read the lines
I cut to feel better
off on their flight
as you also read
those my knife etched
on both forearms
and deemed 'em all
Cliché last class

I left more room
on my upturned wrists
knowing you could kill
making it quick
just an overnighter

You criticized and crossed
all the extra words
I swallowed whole
force-fed to choke
on my own damn pain
that I worked on
to make matters better

You made a poem
painting my dread
superbly written
with your skillsets
I couldn't afford
and you called it
The Mentor.

# Predestined

She is the current-taken jellyfish
Who drags along her tentacles
Each heavily memory-filled
And she drags them on and on
Slowly, weary to keep off
For they will sting even her touch

She is the bride dragging her train
Like fingers scratching the floor
To grab hold and stop her feet
From reaching the wrong altar
But on and on she drags it, still
For the door behind has shut

He is all the weighing memories
That still burn her bearing chest
He is the solemn-standing iceberg
That won't budge an inch her way
So he bears the sunrays' heat
For his trek has long been halted

He is the one who shut the door
Straightening her train, whispering *Go*
He is the weeping willow by the lake
Soon to slide and sink right in
Like terrain thus collapsing
For his roots have long sunken

And I, am the ocean current
That won't change my course
I am the stinging memories
That won't be forgotten
I am the altar's one-way isle
That won't change the groom

I am the weight halting his trek
That won't take him back to her
I am the lake swallowing him
That won't change my tide
I am the one who whispered *Go*
That won't undo my casted curse

Their fate I ended as did mine

# Ash and Smoke

You did not break me
I snapped at you
Making of you a blind man.
If you are the white flag,
Who am I?

You did not crumble me
I became the shards
From beneath your feet.
If you are the toy
Who am I?

You lowered my head
To your filthy feet
But my eyes rose to your neck.
If you are the eyes praising my feet
Who am I?

If you are six feet within me
Begging, banging to get out,
Who the hell am I?

If you are the chin-trembling
Crying coward,
Tell me, damn it, *who* am I?

If…
I've been the train wreck all along
Scraping my knees to the marrow
To stop and hang off your bridge
Knowing you'll also soon crumble,
Who have we become?

Don't look at me like this
I know my tank is hissing.
Save yourself and push me over.
If we've become ash and smoke,

Who was the ignited match?

# A Point in Time

It was never time
To spread a path
Like scattered seeds.
It wouldn't have sprouted
Beyond its point

It was just in time
That we trespassed
The point in time
When space embraced
Our sets of feet

It was splendor instead
Which I found budding
From your pores
That oozed delight
Quick to grasp onto

The point in time
Peaked at dusk
When your pores closed
Catching my fingers
That reached too closely

In every space span
My fingers and yens
Nestled within you.
Caught and released,
I unreadily fell

It was the point in time
To complete the course
Of the Labyrinth of Life
We both walked on
Then left behind

## Backstage Blend

You can't see me like this.
I'd never let you
see the backstage
before the entrance.
All blush and rouge
dabbed on and popped

I'll never be able to fix
these coffee-stained eyes
nor could any powder
hide all of those years.
You see them right here?
And you rubbed them in

I'm better off lip-licking
and cheek-pinching;
coffee-quitting; force-smiling -
slowly genuinely smiling -
a piece of my soul
through a slit in the curtains

Where has yours been?
Your soul stasis and lone
playing the Wise Sage?
while mine tugged on
for yours to join mine
and blend into a Blonde

Removing the milk
the sugar, the cream
and all of the stings
we sipped onto daily.
A pure black blend
savoured backstage

# *Elizabeth*

# Elizabeth's Story

I always remember writing although it wasn't until I wrote my first book starting in 2008 did I collect my thoughts to put them in a book.

I had become a reflexologist in 1996 and started teaching in continuing education classes in both the Catholic and regular school boards. I had to write up a curriculum for the classes and then I also wrote up a hand-out for my students to take away with them in each class. I was always writing something for my students and re-inventing the wheel every time I read another book. Based on my classes, my books came to be and the ideas were hatched in them.

The one thing I can say is that in high school literature class I learned something called précis. At the time, it was just part of what I was doing but I learned to reduce the amount of words I used to describe everything. Even now I edit my writings to do this all the time. I remember my teacher telling me that I wrote very short sentences and maybe I should try to be more descriptive – so far hasn't worked.

I eventually learned so much from writing my books and going out and doing events because of them. Book signings were quite interesting. It was a good thing I was taught to say hello to anyone who came in close range of me. I scared a lot of people but some people stopped and talked to me about my books – not everyone bought one but it was interesting to meet so many people.

Eventually our group, Mississauga Writers Group, was formed and I met more aspiring writers like myself. It has really taught me a lot about what I do. One thing is that I make sure I make decisions which are true to me and I protect what I feel should go into my books.

There were times I said I couldn't write a short story but I was surrounded by short story writers so I did. I have really expanded my horizons within my group and who knows where I will go next but it will be exciting.

# What If?

*by Nicholas J. Banfalvi*

What if there's no light
Only night?
What if you see only grey
Before you could see clearly?
What if there's no justice
Only stealing and killing?
What if there's no love
Only betrayal and hate?

These questions came to me
When you left
I thought we were close
I could smell the roses
I could hear the songs
The birds in the sky sing
The heat of the sun
Is as strong as the heat
of our love
I never said the words
You were waiting for.

What if I said I love you
Would you say the same?
What if you fall for someone else?
What if our love wasn't solid?
What if our love would be there
the next day?

These questions are coming to my head
Oh, the strain of loving can be overwhelming
To know no love
Is like not living
But you are my life
What if you go?
What if life ends too soon?

I can't say the words
Because I'm too sick
I don't want to hold you back
But she still loves me
She really still loves me
I can't believe she still loves me
Don't have to ask the same question "What if?"

## In The Night

The night beckons
It is dark and deep
It holds no sound
and descends on me like a cloak
The crickets chirp
some leaves flutter
The breeze caresses my face
a sickle moon brightly glows
its sounds and sights lay on my senses
The stars twinkle
Their formations rest
Soon the earth will turn
another season will shift
and stars will shift

My life unfolds
In the night's darkness

# Moments

The wind blows
Crickets chirp
Water flows
A door opens
Their eyes at class' end
Nature evolves
Birds chirp
Quiet within
The last moment before I fall asleep
Laughter, giggles
Sudden tears of joy
Loss of a child
Unendurable grief
Memories of three now two
Marriage ends
Silent tears no one sees
To feel love
To touch, to heal
Fear of the unknown
A warm and cozy bed
My home
Alone
Be happy
Flowers' beauty
Wish upon a star

# My Baseball Hopes

My work was going to have a softball game as a friendly get-together for the staff. I had not played softball or baseball in such a long time. I was in primary school when I had played at recess with the other students. We played barehanded in the back school fields. I was always voted as the pitcher because my aim was so good. But that was many years ago.

I asked my 16 year old son to come outside and throw a few balls with me to get me back in the groove. Off we went to the driveway and he started throwing balls to me. I was barehanded but he had a glove on – he was used to it but I had never worn a baseball glove.

Suddenly after a few balls he noticed my right catching hand was getting really red. So he went inside to get a glove for me. Out he came and helped me put it on and make sure it was comfortable. Back he went into position to throw me a ball.

He threw the ball and I caught it in my left hand but the glove was on the right.

"Mom!!!!!" oh, the tables had changed and now he was talking to me in a tone that he would never have accepted from me!

"The glove is on the right hand so you have to catch the ball with your right."

So I threw the ball back and he threw it to me again. I caught it in my left hand.

"Mom!!! You did it again!" Back the ball went and now he was watching me carefully to see how he could teach an old dog a new trick.

Third time catching was still with the left hand. So now he told me to put my left arm behind my back which I did.

He threw it again and I caught it in the glove and then watched the ball fall to the ground.

"Mom!!!! You have to catch it and squeeze the glove to hold the ball." Ok, now it's catch and squeeze! Ok, got it, I think. Back went the ball.

My son threw the ball. I, with my left arm behind my back, caught the ball in the glove and, oh yeah, squeeze. Too bad and too late the ball was already on the ground.

By this time, both my son and I were almost doubled over in laughter. Back went the ball.

He threw it again, I caught it and he yelled "Squeeze" and I almost dropped it but didn't. I was improving.

We did it a few more times and I finally got the "catch and squeeze" concept. We were both almost in tears because we were laughing so hard by this point. My son had to keep yelling "Squeeze" to me each time but I got quicker.

We finally either gave up or relented on my new found baseball prowess. But my son gave me a good idea. He told me he knew which position I should apply for in my futures games. He said I would make a great water-girl or maybe even a bat-girl.

# My Friend Died

My friend Shane died. He was forty, a husband and father and I worked with him for the last twelve almost thirteen years.

You don't know the value of a person until he's no longer there. He was quite a presence at the office – very forceful getting the job done and making his mark. He was there but he was also there for you. He cared about the people he worked with and your station in life wasn't relevant. You were his friend.

Anna, his wife and high school sweetheart, will miss him. It won't matter how many will surround her because he won't be one of them.

His daughters, Ella and Callie, will miss him. Every time they step on the ice at their hockey game, he won't be sitting on the bench opening and closing the door or encouraging them. They'll see their teammates with their fathers but theirs won't be there. Christmas morning will never be the same. The tree, the gifts, the festivities will be forever altered.

At his funeral mass, a thousand people came – unheard of in these times and it was a tribute to the person he was. Childhood friends, fellow workers, family, friends, all came and so many tears were shed. His eulogies from his friends and fellow workers were about the memories of Shane and there were many good and bad. That was the way he was. Tears and laughter accompanied the eulogies. They will miss him.

My friend died and I too will miss him.

# The Couple

They sat in the booth next to me. They were older and looked like they had been married for quite a while. She wore wedding rings but they were an old setting so I knew they weren't modern. He was facing her and I was at a diagonal to him. Her back was to me.

They had just finished breakfast and were finishing off their coffees. It was a small table big enough for their trays and only 2 chairs could fit to the table so their quarters were quite close.

I saw him watching her but I could tell she kept avoiding his eyes. She kept her head down and kept watching her coffee. He kept talking to her but all she did was shrug and not answer. She kept avoiding his looks by turning one way and then the other and looking down at her breakfast remains.

His eyes were soft when he looked at her and I could tell there was no one else in the coffee shop that interested him. She was the only one he wanted to look at and he wanted her attention. She wasn't giving it to him. Her shoulders were slumped and she looked either tired or angry.

I watched them playing their roles – him wanting to make things better and her refusing to acknowledge him. I don't know who was right in this situation but I knew there was trouble. I was divorced for quite a few years and I knew what it was like to be alone at an older age. I watched to see if I could see any fear from her for him but there was none so it was just rejection.

I sat there holding my own cup and watching the scenario unfold. He spoke softly and I could see he was trying to get her attention. He smiled and tried to catch her gaze but she wasn't giving anything to him. He seemed truly trying to smooth out the trouble between them but I could tell she wasn't having any of it. She seemed to reject him more as the time went on.

I tried not to stare but I kept my attention on them. He made several attempts to get her smiling and soften whatever was between them but she didn't relent. At last he sat back and looked out the window to give her space to make up her own mind.

It was sad to see another couple heading for separation maybe not physically but the signs were there. They might live together but apart in their own worlds. They were alone within a marriage and probably still together but unhappy. I thought back on my own marriage and how long I had been there in the same situation. Mine never tried to make peace with me and here was this man trying to right things and smile and get her to just look at him. I felt sad for her. I realize that there were probably a lot of reasons she had to be upset but were they worth it? If you are there, then make the best of it. Mine couldn't be salvaged but in these two I hoped it would be. What I saw in him was only her and the love he felt for her. What I saw in her was hurt or anger and resolution to remain like that. Life is too short to be so incredibly resolved to sadness and upset.

I wanted to call out to her to either resolve the differences or leave but with her would have been the choice to take her unresolved issues with her like we all do.

My coffee was finished and I took one last look at them. He was still staring out the window and so was she. Both were looking at the view and not each other. I could see the sadness in both of them. So close and yet they were so very far away.

I left the coffee shop but I was sad seeing the human torment of being together but apart at the same time.

# The First Date

She stood looking in the mirror. When did she get this old? As if she should be out dating at her age! She straightened her hair and put on her earrings. It had been so long since she had worn earrings. Was her dress right? Did it make her look good? Was it the right colour? Oh, well, it was too late now. She had to go in a few minutes to meet him.

He looked in the mirror. He had shaved very close – wouldn't want to be unshaven when he met her. He looked at himself and wondered what she was thinking. He hoped she would be alright with how he looked. Other women thought he was nice looking. It wasn't as if he couldn't find a woman. Lots of women wanted to date him and more and they were young and cute and oh so willing to have him take them out every night for dinner and spend money on them. What was going to make this woman any different? He checked his watch and knew he needed to leave.

They had met over the internet and had emailed back and forth and he liked how she answered him. She liked what he said and he answered all her questions. She always made sure she asked lots of questions to see if they answered and he did. He had seen her picture and her smile is what captured him. He had put an old picture of himself on the website but he was clean shaven then. She wondered what he thought of her. It wasn't as if she was as slim as the other women she saw around. What was it about her that made him answer her ad? Why did she answer him when he messaged her? She was so pretty and older than him. What could have interested her in him?

They agreed to meet at a local bar with a restaurant attached. At least if they didn't like each other they could just have a drink and some pleasantries and then off they would go on their separate ways. Her single friend always told her to meet her perspective date at a location with lots of people and drive there by herself. This bar is where he always met his friends. He got there, parked and then went inside. What if she didn't look like her picture? He'd met women like that before and he couldn't figure out how they didn't look like their posted picture. He sat at the bar halfway facing the entrance and one foot on the floor in case he had to leave or she didn't show up. He ordered a drink and waited.

She pulled up in her car and parked under a light as her single friend told her. She turned off the car and then just collected her thoughts. What if he didn't look like his picture? It would be a short drink. Her funny expression was that the hardest part of meeting someone was that she had to take a second sip. Oh well, she got out of the car and slowly and anxiously walked into the bar.

Was he there? She looked around and saw one man at the bar halfway facing her but he had a goatee so he wasn't clean shaven. He hadn't arrived yet. She sat at the bar and ordered a fruit juice. She didn't drink so this was the most she got. She was disappointed that he wasn't there yet. What if he didn't show up?

He saw her and knew it was her as soon as she walked in the bar. She stood there and looked around the bar. She was so pretty and was nicer than her picture. The doorway framed her and he couldn't believe his luck. He swallowed and just sat there.

She sat at the bar and noticed the man was watching her. Oh no, don't let him come up to her. She wasn't in the mood to fend off anyone. She just kept watching her drink and every once in a while checked the bar. He called the bartender over and ordered another drink but for her. He let the bartender bring her the drink and he did. Oh no, he actually ordered her a drink and she tried to refuse. He stood up and walked over to her and she stood also. He smiled at her and said her name.

What a relief? It was him. Oh my, and was he ever handsome. He had beautiful blue eyes and they smiled like his lips. She extended her hand in an old fashioned way and he took it. She was so pretty and her smile lit up her face. She had beautiful dark eyes and they sparkled. He held her hand and it was warm and soft in his hand. She held his hand and it was warm and large and held her hand softly but confidently. They introduced each other and then stood for a few seconds not saying anything. He couldn't get over his luck. How lucky was she?

He asked her to sit and they sat beside each other at the bar. They talked easily to each other about their jobs, family and their children but she had grandchildren. She watched him carefully when she spoke of them because of their ages. She wasn't sure this would work out but wanted a night out if for no other reason but to have a handsome dinner companion. He watched her as she talked of her children and grandchildren. Inwardly he sighed. How could this work out?

They enjoyed their drink together and he asked if she would like to go have dinner and she agreed. He felt his hand on her back and wondered why it felt so comfortable. She felt his hand on her back and it was so comforting. He had a way of making her feel comfortable – the first time in a long time for her.

They were seated in a booth with a table between them. They got the menu and he spoke nicely to the waitress. He asked what she liked and it definitely wasn't steak which surprised him because he loved it. He watched as she went through the menu and picked chicken and he picked the steak. The waitress came and he let her order first and then he did.

They sat talking and he laughed at everything she was saying. He laughed so easily and she loved it. There was nothing better than a man who could laugh at her ridiculous sense of humour – he got it all. She was funny and he couldn't remember laughing so much on a date. Their meal came and he made sure she had everything she wanted and they began to eat. He enjoyed his food. He noticed that she enjoyed her food and ate normally. He was so used to women ordering the most expensive dinner on the menu and then picking at it all meal long and leaving more than half and then ordering dessert. She didn't. They ate quietly but spoke between mouthfuls. He said something and she almost spit out her food because she broke out in laughter. He was beginning to know what made her laugh. It was easy.

Their meal was over and they were enjoying coffee and when did they start holding hands over the table? They were holding hands at the end of the booth. He held her fingers in his hand. He held her hand lightly and she liked that. He wasn't assuming anything. What did they talk about? Neither remembered but they talked back and forth easily and laughed often. He played sports and he had so many stories. She had so many stories about her children and grandchildren. He could tell she loved them. He spoke of his children and she could hear the pride in his voice. His were younger and he was still very involved with them.

The time went and they were amazed at the hour. Both had to work the next day – what were they thinking staying out so late. Both had made the date on a week night to ensure they had an excuse to leave early. Now it was well after the time they would be out.

They slowly got up and he took her number. He wanted her to take his but she refused and said she would leave it up to him. How was he going to sleep after the coffee he drank? Unfortunately she had coffee and she knew she was going to be up and sleepless.

They made their way out. He walked her to her car and they stood still talking and laughing for some time later. They looked up at the night sky with the bright moon and stars and it was such a beautiful night. They finally ran out of words and he leaned over and kissed her gently. What a beautiful kiss and so gentle. She was glad that he didn't push it. She needed time to get to know him. What a beautiful kiss. He was glad he did it and he watched and she blushed and lowered her face but then looked up at him. There was a shyness to her.

He started walking away and still they talked back and forth and he stopped often to answer her. Finally he was at his vehicle and both said good night and got into their vehicles. They started them up and each watched the other's back lights. Each started backing out and then he hesitated to watch her and make sure she was alright. She was and then they both drove away slowly their back lights fading the further away they got.

# *Hamzah*

## Hamzah's Story

I found my love for writing in my OAC (Grade 13, no longer exists) English class. Never having been a strong English student, I dreaded receiving what I expected to be another painfully boring assignment. The task was quite different: read an article by Dave Barry, one of the top satirists in the world, and write something along the same lines.

I wrote about a topic that was both personal and ripe for hilarity: being a brown minority in a white-majority city like Burlington, Ontario. I called it *The Brown Times* and judging from people's reactions and their tears of laughter, they seemed to really enjoy it. Over the next few years, I wrote a few sequels to the essay and created a website that featured even more racially-charged satire.

Over the last ten years, as Islamphobia started rearing its ugly head, I realized that the Muslim community needed a good dosage of humour and created a new satire site: *Maniac Muslim*. I quickly learned that comedy could be used as a powerful tool to overcome negative stereotypes and ignorance. The brand exploded in popularity and I was afforded the opportunity to migrate my writing into video and stand-up comedy forms as well, speaking at events, colleges and universities across North America.

I am currently embarking on my latest challenge: a full-length humorous novel entitled *Randomly Selected*.

# The Torn Page

Two friends of mine just died right before my eyes... taken by the She Monster. She's a sociopath, her face filled with diabolical glee as she went on murderous killing spree by taking out my closest childhood friends. I watched helplessly as my two best friends of fourteen years were ripped away from existence... the last sounds they ever heard was the She Monster's shrieking laughter filling the air.

The last week was a particularly bloody one. Five of my compatriots were torn to shreds. There was no reason for this. We are peaceful. We are educators. We aren't violent at all!

We don't know the meaning of violence. How could we be? When you're just a page in a children's book, you sort have to live life as peacefully and family-friendly as possible.

My name is Page 13, though some people call me Page 14.

"Honey," said Page 12, my beautiful wife for as long as I remember, "are you okay?"
"No," I said, fighting back tears, "they're... gone."

"Maybe the worst part is over."
I shook my head slowly. "No honey... the She Monster will ever stop."

We watched the She Monster emerge from her cocoon just two years ago. Her mother was actually a kind soul... it's a wonder how she spawned such a devil-child. The mother used to sit the She Monster on her lap and read our book aloud "The Awesome Book of the Alphabet".

Only problem is we're not really the Alphabet anymore. C, D, G, H, M, N, S, T, W, X and the "About the Author" page are now dead. For the rest of us, our days were numbered.

Who on earth leaves a paper book with a 2-year old She

Monster? I guess it's my own fault... why couldn't I have worked out more and become a board book? Or learned to swim and been a floating bath-time book? I'm jealous of some of my buddies who got promoted to be in a pop-up book. Even when the She Monster inevitably destroys them too, they're at least going out in style.

At this rate, I almost wish I got converted to toilet paper.

"She's coming back!" screamed Page 3. We could hear her pounding footsteps and shrill shrieking getting louder. We were doomed. The remaining pages of the Awesome Book of the Alphabet were screaming.

The book was opening. She was ready for more. So long, page 19 & 20. I never really understood the letter Q and not sure why you always wanted to get with the letter U but I guess you just had a crush on her. Maybe she'll survive all this and –

Never mind, there goes Page 23 & 24 aka U and V. Maybe she can join Q in the Page Afterlife... if that even exists.

Then my heart sank... the She Monster opened our page.

"Honey," said Page 12, turning to me. "I--"

I looked at my wife carefully... I knew this was it. A tear trickled down the page. "I love you," she said... and then I saw my wife being severed.

"No..." I said, hoping this was all just some sick nightmare.

The She Monster cackled, seemingly incapable of having any empathy for anything.

"I'll kill you!" I shouted as I flailed my page the best way I could. It worked. The She Monster stammered back, clutching her hand. I had successfully given her a miniscule paper cut. I could hear her bawling and running out of the room.

The rest of the pages cheered euphorically.

"You did it Page 13!" shouted Page 3, one of the five survivors of the book.

"At a painful cost," I said, looking solemnly at the missing adjacent page.

"I think the She Monster's gone for good," said Page 27.

They cheered again and started up an impromptu celebration… it was the only way to keep sane in this book.

*Thump. Thump. Thump.* The She Monster returned, with a Queen Elsa Band-Aid now placed prominently on her hand. She didn't look like she was happy to see me.

"Uh, guys," I said, as the She Monster clutched my page with vitriol. The other pages stared at me in silence. They knew what was coming. They nodded in salute. I nodded back.

*RIP.*

"Hey, this isn't so bad," I thought, as the She Monster flung me in the air. I was flying and nearly kissed the ceiling. I glided around the flowery pink nursery room, inexplicably at peace with myself. For the first time in my life… I was free.

# How to Salvage a Forgotten Anniversary

1. Acknowledge to yourself that you're a huge screw-up for missing your wedding anniversary. Once you become self-aware of your obliviousness then you can weasel yourself out of any dire predicament in the future.

2. Carefully look into the crestfallen eyes of your spouse. She is probably hurt. This is just the beginning of a volcanic eruption. You will soon hear a lot of words… most of which will insult your intelligence. Embrace them.

3. Stay silent as she proceeds to yell at you for forgetting the most important day in human history: your anniversary. Nod your head occasionally to show that you are listening and not daydreaming about being a professional basketball player.

4. Once her voice becomes hoarse or when her tears have dried up, proceed to tell her that the day isn't over and you have plenty of surprises in store and the whole 'forgetting it was your anniversary' thing was all part of the act. You might need to repeat this a few times before she believes you.

5. After she apologizes for doubting your awesome husband skills, she will start daydreaming this epic anniversary day surprise that you have planned. She now has crazy high expectations for what will probably be a massive disappointment but at least you bought yourself an hour.

6. Make an excuse to run an errand. Pour all the milk in the sink if you have to. It is critical that you are able to leave the house without raising any suspicion or letting her in on the fact that you're making this up as you go.

7. Try to conjure up any pleasant memories you had with her. Was there something she mentioned she liked? Chances are, since you forgot your anniversary, your memory probably can't go back farther than a week at most so trying to figure

out what she wants by using your unreliable noggin is a futile effort.

8.  Using your mobile phone, see if you can login into her Facebook or email and search for any conversations with her friends where they talk about buying things, which might comprise of 95% of all of their conversations. If you don't know your wife's password, try guessing it by putting something she loves the most. If that doesn't work, try putting in your name.

9.  Once you have successfully bought all the things you were supposed to get a week ago, proceed to the floral shop. Flowers are typically the cure to any domestic dispute, no matter how grave. Depending on how severe your wife's wrath was, you might need to consider adding an extra bouquet.

10. Call up your wife and tell her you'll be home soon. Start making vague statements about dinner plans like "Hope you skipped lunch today because I'm taking you to that place that you always wanted to go." Leave a dramatic pause so she can answer. She might take the bait and say something like "You're taking me to that Lakeside Restaurant?" successfully revealing for the first time to you that she indeed wants to go this Lakeside Restaurant. Immediately hang up the call, dial up her choice of restaurant and place a reservation for two. Voila, instant anniversary success.

11. Rinse and repeat for next year.

# *Hans*

# Hans' Story

My younger brother is considered the talented one. Over the decades, while he collected accolades for his fine artistic abilities in painting, sculpture and photography, I just muddled along in the world of day-to-day living; I was not considered creative - practical yes, *but not creative*. My family was mistaken, as I later discovered that I had inherited my father's talent for writing, as well as his love of reading.

I have always enjoyed the English language, with its complexity and richness of variation (and endless possibilities for double entendres!). As the years passed, and I continued to churn out staid reports and essays, I eventually discovered that I had established my own "voice" (that is, a writer's signature style of writing). This development made me reconsider my reluctance to write a work of fiction or some poetry.

Now I recognize and enjoy *my particular creative strength*. Those who once said, "I didn't think you had it in you...," are appreciating the fruits of my labour. I realize that getting lost in "the world of words" is what I do best, and if I approach it honestly and with vigor, there may be much literary gold yet to be mined from within the depths of my subconscious.

## The Torn Page

Unuttered prose,
   A discarded thought –
Rejected confessions,
   Of emotional significance.
Rashly ripped out,
   And tossed aside -
*A torn page,*
   *From the leaves*
*Of my heart.*

# The Interview

Short haircut, clean shave,
      A trimmed mustache apace.
Then the makeup and powder,
      For the horrid pallor of my face.

"First impressions," they say, "are everything."

Pressed slacks, crisp shirt,
      A sharp jacket and tie.
Then polished shoes – my final touch,
      To brand this guy!

"The suit," they say, "makes the man."

Maintain eye contact, I remind myself:
      Stay polite, not "in your face."
Showing arrogance is bad,
      *Do not get put in your place*!

It's not my first interview,
      I've encountered much worse.
Yet I can't seem to shake
      My anxiety, this loathsome curse!
Now panic takes hold,
      I watch in helpless dismay,
While a casket goes down - so slowly,
      Carefully, toward *My* Judgement Day.

With horror I realize, my image contrived,
      Stripped, discarded, and thrown aside.
My soul now stands naked, transparent,
      For all to see – my life was a lie, just a fantasy.

"What a tragedy, what a crime",
      I shriek in dismay.
"What fairness can come,
      If I'm exposed this way?"

What fair-mindedness indeed,
        Other lost souls relate,
While we all anticipate our interview,
        At Saint Peter's Gate.

My turn is now,
        I move up in place,
Catch the old man's eye,
        Smile at his face.
Instead of his mercy,
        Instead of some grace,
Saint Peter, he frowns, turns his back -
        Leaves me there in disgrace.

Suddenly from behind me, comes a chuckle,
        Then a whoop so clear,
As old Satan, the devil,
        Bends in close to my ear.

"Welcome my boy," he growls delightedly.
        "Your actions confirm that you have equaled my best!
Yes, that is right; I have been expecting you,
        Since you so brilliantly passed my test!"

With sinking heart, I realize, the Old Dragon is right:
        *It is during our Lifetime, in all that we do,*
*Where God decides our destiny,*
        *And Humanity's life is its ultimate interview.*

# From Chapter Nine of
## *"THE BLACK SUN ASCENDANT: An Assassin's Tale"*
## *(c.2011)*

Rolling up to the picturesque pastureland fifteen minutes before he was to take flight, Victor found juggling the Blackberry and the bicycle's handlebars a bit tricky. The G.P.S. map display on the Blackberry brought him to a field that turned out to be about a half-an-hour's ride outside of Meiringen.

Victor pulled off the secondary road and onto a dirt path that wound around the circumference of a pasture. He scanned the field for any sign of a helicopter. Surrounded by groves of trees that cast long shadows in the fading evening light, he could see no sign of the aircraft. Guessing that one of the pools of deep shadow helped to conceal the helicopter, Victor decided to begin his search around the tree line of the pasture.

Leaving the bicycle leaning against a tree and pocketing the Blackberry, it wasn't long before Victor stumbled onto the helicopter, almost running face first into the dark olive green of the tail fin. Eleven feet high and six to seven feet wide not counting the rotor, its nose was the shape of a cut diamond and there was no sign of external weaponry. This was Victor's first introduction to a Comanche RAH-66 and he was impressed.

"Guten Abend Vater (Good evening Father). Darf ich Ihnen behilflich sein (May I help you)?" came a greeting from the tree-side of the helicopter. The pilot, American by his accent, looked no more than twenty-seven, athletic and about five-eight in height with a severe buzz cut and clean-shaven. He wore the typical olive colored flight suit and held his helmet in his left hand while the right clutched a cigarette.

Victor, who wore the clerical outfit from earlier in the day and exchanged the hiking breeches for black slacks, flashed a smile in the young man's direction.

"I speak English, if it would be easier for you. My name is Father Anthony Ricci. Are you giving rides to the Vatican?"

"Sure am! So you're the fellow I'm supposed to fly in on the QT." A broad smile broke out on the pilot's face, "I'm Gordon Chambers, at your service".

"How long do you think the flight will take and can you really get us into Vatican City?"

"Sneaking onto the Vatican property with this bird shouldn't be a problem. The flight will take from two to two-and-a-half hours depending on the weather and if we've a head or a tail wind. I've logged our flight plan with Rome's Fiumicino Airport, so they think we'll be making our way there as a private jet. An hour-and-a-half into our trip we'll drop off their radar and they'll never know where we've gone. By the time they begin the search you've been dropped off and I'm out of there." He stopped to take another puff of the cigarette, "Weather's cleared up nicely since this morning, hasn't it Father?"

It did not take long to buckle Victor into the weapons officer's seat and strap on his helmet. The young pilot then tested Victor's communications and oxygen supply. Readying himself, the pilot lowered and locked the helicopter's canopy and within a few minutes Victor heard the chopper's rotors begin to turn.

With a flick of the switch, the inside of Victor's visor suddenly glowed with a 'heads-up' display.

"What you're seeing is the H.S.I. or horizontal situation indicator, that tells us where we're pointed in relation to the ground," the pilot said, his voice breaking into Victor's thoughts through the helmet's earphones. "And on your left you've got the speed, on the right the altimeter. At the bottom is the yaw or side-to-side motion, while at the top of the heads-up you see the compass and G.P.S. coordinates. Hold onto your stomach, Father!"

As he said this, the helicopter leaped up from the ground at an amazing rate, faster than anything he had ever experienced at any amusement park. The ground seemed to Victor to be receding faster than the sun could sink behind the horizon.

"How fast are we rising and at what altitude will we be flying?" Victor asked.

"I'll bring the climb up to 800 feet per minute and we'll level off at about 8,500 feet; higher than 10,000 feet and we'll need oxygen. The Furkapass, through which I'm flying, is just over 7,000 feet so we should have lots of clearance. Once we've crossed into Italy I'll bring her down to 5,000 feet. Our cruising speed will be 161 knots or about 192 miles an hour. How's your stomach holding out Father?"

"Fine thanks!" Victor replied, smiling grimly to himself as he remembered Reg's remark about how fun the flight would be. Too bad about Reg - he had been a good friend, someone Victor could rely on in a business where you never knew who to trust.

The night came quickly as they flew from Switzerland over the Alps into northern Italy. Once on Italy's west coast, the chopper turned south to fly along the eastern edge of the Ligurian Sea. Victor could clearly see the difference between the scattered, bobbing lights of the sea going vessels on his right and the steady, land-based lights of homesteads and villages on his left.

Unexpectedly, Victor felt the helicopter's forward motion translate downwards. The shoreline seemed to rush up to meet them.

"Here's where we disappear Father! I'm switching over to the night-vision, pilotage system. I'm also turning on the radar jamming equipment to ensure complete stealth. Just below us is the small town of Tarquinia, where we're turning inland to make our approach to Vatican City."

"How close to the ground do you intend to go?"

"I'll be flying no higher than 75 feet, Father," the pilot said.

At this low altitude, Victor could clearly see the roads, farm fields and buildings zip by below, while the greenish glow of his night vision system gave everything an 'other-worldly' appearance. Now over open land, the pilot flew the chopper even closer to the ground; Victor guessed they were not more than twenty feet in the air. The aircraft rose and fell, moving from side to side, undulating over the contours of the land based features - he felt as though locked onto the rails of an imaginary roller coaster.

"We're flying what you pilots call 'nap-of-the-earth,' is that right?"

"That's right Father, you've done your homework!"

Victor could hear the elation in the pilot's voice; he was having the time of his life, Victor thought. Glancing at his watch, Victor noticed that it was just 10 o'clock. The stars in the night sky twinkled in the clear heavens overhead as the landscape flew past in the greenish, ethereal blur. Victor knew he had guessed correctly about the overland route they were flying when the land gave way to a large expanse of water not fifteen feet below them.

"That's Lake Bracciano," the pilot confirmed, as if reading Victor's thoughts. "We'll be at the Vatican in another few minutes. It's been a pleasure flying with you Father."

"The pleasure was all mine young man. You've been a most congenial host."

*****

**Vatican City, Rome, same time.**

While Janet, Sarah and the two men of the Kidon team

scrambled to pack up their office before the next day's noon deadline, an urgent burst of radio traffic came out of the Vatican's security office next door. Ever curious, the two Mossad agents decided to poke their heads into the office and find out what the commotion was.

"Radar installations all around Rome and the surrounding countryside are down. The airports have had to tell the incoming flights to stay in a holding pattern until further notice and all outgoing flights have been canceled for now. The Aeronautica Militare has scrambled a team of Panavia Tornados to try to find the source of the interference. Police and military ground forces are also combing the streets, looking for the potential problem."

"How long has the radar been down?" Sarah asked.

"For almost an hour now. The authorities are beginning to worry," the security officer replied.

"Anything else affected?"

"Nothing at the..." As he began to speak the bank of video monitors in front of him, showing all areas of Vatican City, turned to snow. The radio receivers behind him dissolved into white noise. "Oh, merda!" the guard shouted as he pushed past Janet and Sarah, racing down the hall to his supervisor's office.

"Let's get our team out to the administration building to see Cardinal Richter," Janet suggested to Sarah. "I know that meeting with him again is not the most pleasant of ideas, but with this latest development we might get an extension at the Vatican allowing us to finish our investigations."

"Okay, if you think it's really necessary," Sarah grudgingly agreed, while stifling her feelings of misgivings.

Ahu sat on a small stone bench and had a good cry, oblivious to the beauty of the Vatican Gardens at night. She had had no luck in obtaining an interview with Cardinal Richter after three days of attempts; she felt her name had become anathema at the Vatican. Now ten-thirty on a Tuesday evening, Ahu slipped into the Vatican gardens to have some privacy. She tried to settle her rattled nerves and formulate a new plan of action now that her last chance of gaining an audience with the Cardinal had slipped away. Unfortunately, the only things that came easily were tears, three pent-up years' worth of them shed for Fehime and every other emotional tragedy that had followed her friend's death. The mask of a stoic crusader had slipped off to reveal how emotionally raw she felt inside herself.

Cardinal Richter, meanwhile, was working another late night. He realized he needed a brief stroll around the Vatican gardens for renewed invigoration, before another attack on the pile of paperwork that cluttered his desktop.

Entering through the Courtyard of the First Martyrs, he walked up the main path. Dotting it at intervals, amber pools shed their glow from ornate light standards along the path's border. Striding quietly onward, he noticed the night air filled with the sounds of sirens, aircraft and ...and what? Was it crying? With Rome in such chaos, he wondered, what did the good Lord have planned for his flock tonight?

"Cardinal Richter? Is that you Prime Minister?" Victor, amazed at his good luck, had never stumbled on a target as easily as he did tonight.

"Yes? Who is there?" Richter demanded. Upset to find his peace interrupted, Cardinal Richter now wished he had taken his personal security escort with him.

Victor stepped from the shadows into a pool of light shed by one of the path's lamps; his facial features thrown into sharp contrast to the surrounding darkness. Richter moved in for a closer look.

"Oh Father, I'm sorry, you startled me. Please excuse my abruptness. What is your name?"

"Father Anthony Ricci, Prime Minister, it is a distinct pleasure to meet you." Victor held out his hand and the Cardinal grasped it firmly.

"It's rather late to be walking in the gardens, don't you think Father?" Richter asked.

"I'm a night owl, Prime Minister. I've always had trouble sleeping."

Ahu, who had chosen one of the garden alcoves in which to sit, overheard the two men's conversation taking place on the other side of the high privet hedge. The voice of Father Ricci sounded so familiar - where had she heard it before? Moving stealthily, she soon found a thin place in the hedge affording a clear yet discreet view of the path where the two men stood. What she saw next startled her.

"...Just so, I've heard that these particular liturgical studies are very good Father Ricci and Father Vanier is an able teacher. But now I won't hold you up any further Father." Richter was about to leave when Victor grabbed the Cardinal by the arm, dropping his pretense as a priest.

"Not so fast Prime Minister!" Victor's tone grew cold, menacing. "Do you have any idea why someone would want you dead?"

Shocked, Richter went on the attack, "What in the name of God are talking about Father?"

"I've been sent to kill you Cardinal, and I'd like to know why. Who did you upset enough to have them want you assassinated?"

Ahu's blood went cold. The face, the voice, it was James Glasgow - the man she loved! What could he mean by saying that he had come to kill the Cardinal? Frozen to her spot on the opposite side of the hedge, all she could do was watch this bizarre exchange unfold.

"I don't know what you are talking about," Richter snapped. "I'm going to have you arrested." Trying to turn away again, Richter felt Victor's powerful grip pull him back, bringing him face-to-face with the assassin's Glock automatic.

As fear gripped Richter, his knees turned to jelly. "So...so it's not the Pope...," he stammered.

"What's not the Pope? What are you talking about Richter?"

"The contract was not for the Pope's life, it was for mine!" Richter's eyes met Victor's; they seemed to be pleading with Victor for mercy.

"Tell me again Cardinal, why would someone want you dead?"

"I don't...I don't know..."

Victor noticed the lack of sincerity in the Cardinal's voice, but before he could begin to play rough with the man, a shout came from the entrance to the Vatican Gardens.

"Hold it, put down your weapon Mr. Glasgow!" The Mossad assassin, taking an educated guess in using Victor's alias, pointed the 22 caliber Beretta in Victor's direction.

Hearing this use of his alias, Victor instinctively shifted his position to just behind the Cardinal, whose back was to the Mossad agent.

The Mossad assassin saw a brief opportunity at a clear shot and took it, unleashing a slew of bullets from his Beretta. The opportunity had been too brief; however, and he ended up hitting the Cardinal, not Victor. As the Cardinal slumped forward, Victor used his body as a shield and returned fire, landed a direct hit on the assassin and killing him instantly.

Ahu heard the name Glasgow, then the shots rang out and she saw the Cardinal crumple to the ground while James fired back at the unseen shooter. She almost cried out in horror. To see James firing a weapon had shattered every precious ideal she had built up about him since their time together. Now emotionally spent, and physically paralyzed with fear, Ahu slipped to a sitting position on the ground while Death paid a visit to the men on the opposite side of the hedge.

The quiet had returned to the Vatican's garden and two men lay prostrate on the ground, while Victor remained kneeling beside the Cardinal's body surveying the carnage. Still barely alive, the Cardinal beckoned Victor to come closer. Leaning over the priest's mouth while still gripping his gun, Victor listened to the man's last confession.

"The...the secret...cough, cough..." Richter gurgled, blood trickled from his mouth.

"What secret?" Victor asked.

"The secret lies...cough...lies beneath a Casa...cough...a Casa in Toronto...haaaaaaa." Richter's eyes glazed over and his head rolled sideways as his breath left his body.

"Toronto? Toronto, Canada? Damn you Richter!"

Victor heard the shout of a woman's voice cry 'no,' then felt an explosion inside his head. There was a period of blinding light and a pain like the feeling of a white-hot poker tearing its way through the right side of his temple. Finally, unconsciousness swept Victor up into its dark, anesthetized embrace and his body fell limply over Richter's.

Ahu, too afraid to look at the growing bloodshed on the other side of the hedge, had heard everything. She would never forget this night.

Coming from the direction of the Vatican administration building, Janet, Sarah and the other Mossad assassin had heard the shots fired in the Vatican Gardens. They saw their Mossad man dead on the path. Janet then cried out as the remaining assassin took aim and fired at Victor; she just managed to jog the assassin's arm, and threw his shot off course. As Victor's body lay atop the dead Cardinal, Janet turned to the remaining Mossad assassin.

"You fool," screamed Janet, "he's no good to us dead! I just hope to God you didn't kill him."

Janet ordered the Kidon agent to grab Victor and place him in the back seat of their car.

Meanwhile she and Sarah struggled to lift the body of the dead Mossad assassin into the trunk of the vehicle. The three then got in, drove out of Vatican City, and disappeared into the heart of Rome.

Ahu, sobbing quietly, remained alone with the corpse of Cardinal Richter. Privy to all that had gone on and noticed by no one, she remained on the ground, knees tucked under her chin, rocking gently back and forth while melancholy remained her only companion.

### *End of Black Sun Bk1 excerpt.*

# From Chapter Fourteen of
## *"AN EARTH ECLIPSED: An Assassin's Revenge" (c.2015)*

Victor Colvin's charter landed at Sochi International Airport, and he was glad for the break in the tedium. The long, uneventful flight had given him time to think, and think he did. How lucky he had been to reconnect with a trusted contact still living in an old, Cold War era apartment complex near the center of Moscow. Victor was luckier still to find that she still carried a torch for him, and as a sign of faith, had kept the sealed package he had given her so many years ago in hopes of his return. Unbeknownst to her, the package was an emergency drop - an extra change of clothes, new passports and identification papers and money, lots of money; some of which he gave to her as a 'thank you'.

Picking up the small Fiat that his Moscow companion had arranged for him, it was not long before Victor, now masquerading as Jonathan Rampart, was driving south toward the resort town of Sochi. Below him lay the shimmering expanse of the Black Sea and its hectic flurry of shipping traffic. To the town's north and east sat the Caucus Mountains with their verdant, forested slopes topped by brilliant snow-capped peaks.

Coughing its way to the center of town, Victor pointed the vehicle toward Sochi's southwestern edge, and the Russian presidential dacha. His meeting with Adel was long overdue.

### Gardens of the Russian Presidential retreat, Sochi, Russia.

Higher, and ever higher I soar as powerful updrafts flow beneath my wings. The ground quickly recedes and my view explodes into a brilliant panorama where, at this altitude, the air is very thin and bitingly crisp.

My focus remains only on the distant, tiny specks below as I 'wait on'. My sharp eyesight searches for my prey. Earthward, a sudden fluttering, erratic movement, and splash of white that careens away from my handlers tells me it is time to act - my quarry is released!

From tranquil to tense, heart pumping rapidly, I am supplied with the energy I need, as my eyes lock onto my target and I fall into 'the stoop'. I, rushing downward and never wavering, come swiftly closer, though the poor creature I am after flies its desperate course in hopes of saving itself. The blast of air past my feathers, sliding over my aerodynamic form, sends a charge of excitement through every fibre of my being. Flying is what I was born to do! All around me becomes a blur as I accelerate my dive and sharpen my perspective on my hapless victim.

Extending my legs, with talons outstretched and glistening in the sunlight, I prepare for the catch. A jog to the left, a sudden right, and a dive up then down; the poor creature I am chasing is no match for me. One swift snatch and its fleshy body at first struggles, then falls limp, held fast in my secure grip. In sheer exaltation, I push myself higher and then, dropping my speed, move in long, languorous arcs across the beautiful blue firmament. Far below I see it raised and beckoning, the fist of my master holding my reward for such a fine capture; it is my command to descend back toward the Earth.

"Excellent catch, Prince," Grigorivich said as he approached Sheikh Badr Bahadur Abd-al-Aziz's small hunting party.

The falcon settled comfortably on the heavy leather gauntlet protecting the Prince's left hand, while an assistant moved carefully forward to remove the corpse of a snow-white dove from its talons. He took great care not to startle the sensitive bird as it tore at a large piece of raw beef that Abd-al-Aziz gripped tightly between the fingers of his gauntleted hand.

"Thank you, Mr. President, yes, she is an excellent hunter – the best I have among my host of falcons." The Sheikh cast an admiring glance over the crow-sized bird.

Taking a step closer, Grigorivich tried to get a better look at the fine young hunter when she suddenly flinched and spread her wings, squawking out her warning not to approach.

"Please, Mr. President, may I ask you to keep your distance." The Sheik held his falcon more firmly by her jesses, "These birds are highly excitable and appreciate only the proximity of their familiars."

"Of course, Prince, my apologies," Grigorivich replied, backing away and giving a sidelong glance to his assistant, Ioanin Rostislav. "I've come personally to let you know that dinner will be in approximately one hour, and that we will assemble in the library for the introductions. I hope that all is well with your accommodations?"

As the Prince made a slight bow, the late afternoon sun caught the silken threads in his dark robes and made them glisten. "I am most satisfied, Mr. President, with your hospitality towards my small party."

Rostislav inadvertently grunted aloud upon hearing the word 'small' in relation the Abd-al-Aziz's entourage. Twenty-five people in all including the falcon handlers and security detail had stretched the dacha's accommodations to the limit, forcing some of its staff to relinquish their rooms and stay in Sochi. A quick, withering glance from Grigorivich forced his officer to look down and step further into the background.

Ignoring the insolence of the employee, Sheikh Abd-al-Aziz turned and handed his noble raptor to his nearest falconer. The man accepted it, and immediately placed a small, leather hood over the bird's head that immediately quieted it. The group of falconers then turned and walked back to the dacha and the location of the bird's pen.

Returning his attention to Grigorivich, who had been watching the handling of the great bird with much interest, Abd-al-Aziz continued, "I look forward to your soiree, Mr. President, and until then, 'May Allah be with you.'" The Prince bowed and then proceeded toward the dacha with his security detail in tow and leaving the two Russians alone, standing in the middle of the retreat's extensive gardens.

Grigorivich glanced at Rostislav, his steel gray eyes narrowing as he cautioned his employee, "Ioanin, watch yourself around our guests, especially the Prince. To offend any of them now would be a great loss to Russia's coming fortunes!"

"Da (Yes)," the ex-Major grumbled, and then said, "I'll double check the outside perimeter of the presidential compound, Sir."

"Fine, Ioanin, fine, I'm going to change for dinner, then check with you again before I see the guests."

Sitting high up and well concealed in the foliage of a copse of trees just outside the perimeter wall of the Russian President's compound, Victor Colvin watched intently as the Sheikh's falcon performed its acrobatic display. He also saw the brief exchange between Grigorivich and the Prince, and then the departure of the Sheikh and his entourage toward the presidential dacha.

Comfortably planted on a sturdy branch twenty feet above the ground, Victor relaxed to the rhythmic roar of the Black Sea waves as they rolled onto the shore behind him. The salty/sweet fragrance of sea air and spring blooms blew gently on the warm northerly breeze, encouraging him to remove his jacket and roll up his sleeves. Through the field glasses, he watched as the two Russians parted ways. The taller more handsome Grigorivich turned toward the dacha, while Ioanin Rostislav moved in the direction of the estate's rear most perimeter gate, then through it to the outer security perimeter.

Victor followed Rostislav's movements as the Russian picked his way carefully through the thick vegetation that grew outside the high walls of the compound bordering the Park Rivyera. While he gazed through the binoculars, the assassin's mind drifted back to Adel's last text message to the team, "Meet presidential dacha, Sochi, a.s.a.p." For 48 hours now, she had ignored his prompt for more information and he hoped that she was not in any trouble.

As the Russian security man's powerful frame made its appearance through a thicket of shrubs, Victor carefully picked his way back down from his perch and landed lightly on the ground. It was time, he thought; time to get this assignment back on track.

Ioanin Rostislav continued his walk along the outer wall of the presidential compound, and looked for anything suspicious on the park side of the barrier. Grumbling as he clawed his way through an unusually tangled group of shrubs, he made a mental note to remind the staff to re-cut the security perimeter around the outer wall. He would have some strong words for the groundskeeper when he got back inside the compound - a thought that held more relish for him as he unexpectedly caught his foot on an exposed root and stumbled out of a thicket and into a clearing.

Rostislav had reached the southernmost point of the presidential compound where its wall jutted into the Rivyera Park and was closest to the thicket of trees where Victor Colvin lay hidden. The Russian then glanced up to see the position of the perimeter's cameras, and reassured that they would not see him, he quickly ducked into the thicket, while withdrawing his automatic from its holster. Cocking his head to one side, the ex-Major swivelled his thick neck, straining to hear anything that might be out of the ordinary. The only sounds he heard were the rustling of leaves and myriad of bird song in the trees, the roar of the surf on the nearby shore and the occasional bark of the security dogs inside the compound. Relaxing his composure, he let the hand holding the weapon fall to his side.

"Hello Ioanin, thanks for coming," the assassin said, keeping his voice low in case a foot patrol on the dacha side of the wall overheard him.

Startled, Rostislav turned in the direction of the voice, swinging his Taurus 9mm up and pointing it in Victor's direction. Slowly advancing into a pool of sunlight, the shadow disappeared from the assassin's face and the Russian broke into a broad smile of recognition. Holstering his gun, he raised his arms and gave a bear hug to Victor Colvin.

"Hello my friend, it has been a long time since we last met!" he said in a loud whisper, his thick accent almost swallowing each word. "It is good to see you looking so well. When I got your message I was suspicious…but it's really you – thank God in all his mercy."

"I see you still have the Taurus I gave you – how you like it?"

Removing it again from the holster, the Russian held the automatic up to the sunlight where its brushed metal gleamed. Victor noticed how well the molded grip seemed to blend with the man's beefy right paw.

"I don't go anywhere without it, my friend, it is my lucky charm," the security man said. "Of all the women I have ever known, this is the one that has felt the most natural in my hands; and has been the most useful!" He chuckled at his own joke and Victor himself could not help smiling, knowing the hell the Russian had been through just to save his own life.

"I hope you understand Ioanin that I couldn't stay with you that afternoon, I had to leave before your people arrived."

"Still Victor," Rostislav began, leaning heavily on a hard 'c' in Victor's name, "you saved my life – that was enough for me. Pulling me out of that fire and leaving me sheltered with this sweet mistress…" He caressed the nine-millimeter again then holstered it. "It was enough to allow me to protect myself until help arrived. I owe you, my friend."

"I couldn't leave you unprotected, especially with the rebels still crawling all over that village."

"Da (Yes)…" Rostislav said, and Victor noticed a wistful expression come into the ex-Major's eyes as he recalled that fiery day in a Chechen battle zone. Victor was there, hired by the Russian authorities to take out an important, and heavily guarded enemy general. Stumbling through the surreal scene, dodging both friendly and enemy fire, the assassin came across the then Captain trapped and semi-conscious in the wreckage of a tank. He had obviously been trying to get out of the immobilized vehicle when a second artillery shell pounded it, driving a piece of the metal plating through the man's right thigh and pinning him to the burning hulk of metal.

On hearing the man's cries as he struggled to dislodge the shrapnel from his leg, Victor realized it would not be long before the fire would do its work and roast the poor fool alive. Jumping onto the tank and suffering burns himself for his trouble, he helped the semi-conscious soldier to freedom, moving him to a more sheltered spot and away from the battlefield's main action.

Quickly patching up the soldier's wounds as best he could, Victor then left the man with the nine-millimeter Taurus and some remaining clips of ammunition. The assassin then disappeared into the chaos, never expecting to see this fellow again, but for his own sake, hoping that his people would find him before the enemy did.

Years later, Victor Colvin stumbled onto a news article telling about the man whom he had saved so many years ago. It spoke of how Ioanin Rostislav had become not only a war hero of Russia, but also the Security Chief to the Russian President; Victor realized he now had an important connection to the Kremlin.

The light was beginning to fade as evening began to draw in on the two men in that copse of trees. This suited them fine, though Rostislav knew he did not have much more time – he would have to make a final report to the President before the evening's festivities began. Victor Colvin realized as much and went straight to business.

"Ioanin, I contacted you because I need your help."

"Name it my friend," the other man growled.

"First, do you have a gun for me?"

In answer, the Russian reached into the small of his back and pulled out a Glock automatic. From an inner pocket of his windbreaker, he pulled out a silencer and two magazines of ammunition. "I hope you won't have to use them here," he said, jerking his thumb in the direction of the presidential compound.

"I agree," Victor replied, accepting the items. "My primary reason for being here is to contact the young woman with whom the Russian President is currently sleeping."

"What! That little mink, the one who calls herself Adel Pikantnova, she's with you?" The ex-Major's eyes brightened in an uncharacteristic show of merriment that Victor would not have thought possible for the man.

"Well yes, in a manner of speaking, she is. I've got to see her and I need your help to get me into the compound unnoticed."

Still chuckling to himself, the Russian held out his hand and wrapped his meaty paw around Colvin's grip. "I owe you my life, my friend," he repeated, "Others would have left me to burn alive in that Chechen Hell-hole, but you risked your own life to get me out…"

"Technically we were on the same side," Victor interrupted, "I had an obligation to help…" Rostislav cut him short with a wave of his hand. Even in the day's fading light the assassin could see the sincerity blazing in the Russian's eyes.

"I must go or they will begin to wonder where I am. Be by the rear gate at eight-o-clock tonight. I'll make sure that it is unlocked and the area clear, but it can only be so for five minutes; more than that and an alarm will sound!" With that Rostislav gave Victor a final, hearty handshake, "Goodbye my friend." Then turned and strode to the edge of the thicket where he stopped, took a quick, critical look around and slipped back into the remainder of his perimeter tour.

*End of Black Sun Bk2 excerpt.*

# Abridged Interview with Jasmine Sawant, March 2015

Here follows an abridged interview with Jasmine Sawant, a member of the Mississauga Writers Group and active author, actor, manager and director:

1. **Were you creative as a child, and if so, which side of the family did you get if from?**
   I don't think I was as creative or skilled as my mother, but I definitely get it from her. My mother was highly educated for a girl of her times born into a family of farming landowners - she had a B. A. in History and Political Science. She was born in 1932 in a village with one main street and two back streets and a cluster of small houses. Girls in those days, cooked, cleaned, sewed, embroidered, [in] all of which my mother excelled.

2. **What was your preferred creative past time? What was it in your upbringing, family/social environment that may have led to your being so creative now, as an adult?**
   I was a dreamy child who only liked to read. [I would] escape into magical worlds on my own and, when I had a couple of kids to play with, create a make-believe world with whatever was at hand. A pot, pans, scraps of fabric, blocks of wood, sticks, stones, etc. I loved to dress up and pretend to be one of those characters that I had made up, influenced by my readings, no doubt. Nevertheless, I did not have too many kids to play with [and] my sibling was [only] a baby then, so it was like being an only child.

   I grew up in a suburb of Bombay (now Mumbai), and at my mother's insistence, was enrolled into a convent school, where the medium of instruction was English right from Junior Kindergarten. She insisted that we speak English...this made for a lonely childhood, [since], in the building where we lived, people spoke only in their mother tongues, and children went to schools that taught in those languages, not in English. [This] solitude meant that I read a lot, and used my imagination to create more verbal stories that I could act out, whenever I had an opportunity.

3.  **Was there something about the countries in which you lived that necessitated your creative yearnings?**
    I did not physically leave India until I was married and already had my first child. However, [during] all [those] years…in India, my reading took me all over the world. I liked reading fiction and non-fiction as well as historical/political works; geography was one of my favourite subjects at school. I liked poring over maps, reading quaint facts about distant lands. I loved reading about scientists and their discoveries and the sacrifices they had to make to achieve what they did. I loved mysteries, especially Sherlock Holmes, thrillers, romances, and fairy-tales. I had written a fairy tale and sent it to a children's magazine, but got my rejection letter and was so dejected that I did not write any more. That was when I was in middle school.

    I took up Journalism and then studied French at the Alliance Francaise. I loved reading Moliere's plays and writers such as Balzac, Guy de Maupassant, Jean Paul Sartre, and Albert Camus. Later I studied German [and] was not very excited about Goethe or Schiller, but I did like Bertolt Brecht. While in Mumbai, I worked for a short while in the cultural department at Goethe-Institute. After we moved to Bahrain, I took up a job at the French Embassy.

4.  **How important, in your opinion, is it to promote creativity in any of its forms in children, and is it fair for some parents to stifle such creativity in favour of the "more practical" pursuits?**
    Parents should let their children's imagination soar. Curbing that inhibits creativity. I do not vehemently protest if parents want their children to pursue practical/useful fields of study, but don't stop them from following creative/artistic activity either. Let their imagination run wild, all within the parameters of personal and public safety of course. At some point the child, at his/her young adult

stage will make a choice. Having been part of both the creative and practical, he/she will be better informed to make a smart career choice that is his/her own. Parents will be pleasantly surprised by their children's choices. In today's world no one really wants to be that 'impoverished artist in the garret'. Many times parental opposition fuels unnecessary arguments resulting in rebellion.

5. **Your website advertises you as an "actor, producer, writer, manager". Which of these four designations do you value most and why?**
Being an avid reader, writing was but the next step. One of my dreams, as a young girl was to see my name in the byline, or as author of a novel. That novel is still in the wings, waiting, but seeing my name as playwright was exciting! The actor followed the writer. I was painfully shy. The moment I got up on stage, as myself, I had all the symptoms: dry mouth, pounding in my ears, thumping in my chest, a fine film of sweat on my brow, etc. The moment I was playing a character, I was fine. That was not me, and I could say and do all that the character demanded. I loved that.

For my theatre company, I can't afford to hire an administrator. People love to volunteer to be an actor, sometimes provide technical support, or help run an event only on the day of the event itself. Sadly, but not surprisingly, no one likes to volunteer to carry out routine administrative tasks. I have a vision for my theatre company, and for that, I am willing to take on all those tasks too. It's worth it. I have to try to realize this dream that I have, or die trying.

6. **How does motherhood and marriage influence your choice of acting roles, or writing topics? Do you think that this important aspect in your life has added depth and meaning to what you do creatively?**
Marriage and motherhood both influence my choices, but motherhood has the more lasting impact. They not only add

depth and meaning, but also profoundly affect how I think. My theatre group produces and presents women-centric plays. For example, on the topic of war, the protagonists are usually men, and…such stories usually focus on the heroism, the loss, the heroic sacrifices, but from a woman's perspective, and moreover as a mother, this focus sharpens to the ill effects of war generally and more personally, it is the futility of losing one's young son or daughter in unnecessary bloodshed. For a mother, that is a story that's very important, and needs to be told.

7. **How important is your husband's, and children's' endorsement of what you do on stage and on paper?**
Very! They have to believe in it even though it may not be to the extent that I do. And if they don't agree, I spend hours discussing my viewpoint, so they do endorse it eventually ☺.

8. **In your creative work as an actor or writer, do you feel compelled to send a message with each piece that you do, or can you perform something that merely entertains?**
It's possible to have 'just entertainment'. 'Just entertainment'…usually has the largest audience and the highest ticket prices. This makes it very difficult to market my plays, since I feel compelled to have a message with every piece. I don't like the message to be 'in your face', but it has to be a clear message. Many of the plays that I produce are also on uncomfortable topics, and many audience members may not find that entertaining. That does not mean I shun entertainment. That has to come through humour in the script: dark, dry, subtle, or situational.

9. **What type of writing does the "writer" part of you like to pursue – poetry, short/long fiction, non-fiction or something that aids you as an actor, like plays?**
Plays come more easily to me so that's what I have done so far. Usually there's a social message, or a romantic story with an underlying message. I start seeing scenes and hearing dialogue in my mind to convey that message, and

that's how it begins. I have started some short fiction, but have not completed it. Moreover, I do want to do a long fiction piece, but am waiting to retire…before I start that. I love poetry…it moves me profoundly; the emotions, imagery and the succinct way [in] telling it, but I don't think I am a poet, though sometimes I write rhyming verse☺.

10. **What type of writing would you like to try, but may be afraid to approach because you perceive it as difficult? How do you think that you can overcome it; perhaps through mentoring, like you had in acting in 1975, while in India?**
I would love to work with a mentor, on both long fiction and non-fiction. I also want to do a screenplay. The screenplay I am afraid to take on, but have been researching courses.

11. **Is the transition from actor to writer, and back again, difficult?**
I prefer not to act in plays that I have written. The writer in me is too strong to take a back seat, so I direct what I write, and…do not act. It would actually be wise not to direct what I write. It is more exciting to discover someone else's treatment of what one has written, provided the essence of the message is not changed.

12. **Do the people you work with feed your creativity, and do you think that you give something to them other than just playing their producer/manager/director?**
Some inspire me more so than others, but mostly you end up working with the same people because they are inspirational and together you are able to create something beautiful. I have been told that I, or the process of being in one of my productions, has been inspirational to some. I am saying that with authority as I have these beautiful messages in writing☺. I would not automatically assume that I have been inspiring.

13. **Where do you see yourself taking your personal creative career in the future? Do you want more "fame" (for lack of a better term)?**

If I want fame for myself, I should be trying my luck in Bollywood not struggling with a small theatre company. What I am trying to achieve is big…there is no precedent for it in Mississauga; it is creating something without having recourse to roadmaps. I want to establish South Asian theatre that is meaningful, professionally produced, and ongoing, in some of the languages of that part of world, including English. I want the Eastern and Western influences to meld in the fields of acting, production values, etc. At the same time, I want the stories to be South Asian in context, relevance, appeal, characterization, etc. [Moreover], there has to be 'heart' in what one does, always.

14. **Is the dance company you manage, *Lata Pada SAMPRADAYA Dance Creations*, your primary concern for now, and for the near future? Do you see it as a national or international success?**

Sampradaya Dance Creations is a successful company at all levels, local, national, and international. I like my work there, my boss, Lata Pada is hugely inspirational and supportive of my theatre company, so I will be there for some time. It does put some of my writing plans on hold. I don't like that, but then, one can't have everything…

15. **Have you performed in, or written for this company? How important is it to you, that western audiences be exposed to this exquisite form of eastern dance style?**

I am not a dancer, so I have not performed for Sampradaya Dance Creations, but I have written a dance-theatre piece for children, titled "One World Our World" which Sampradaya Dance Academy, the sister concern of Sampradaya Dance Creations, performed in 2010 and remounts it in June 2015 to celebrate their 25th anniversary. It's a kind of a fairytale with messages on the dangers of messing with one's environment. It's a feel good story and highlights environmental issues both in the past and present and in India as well as Canada.

16. *Why are you creative* – **what does it do for you and what does it mean to you in your busy life as career woman, wife, and mother?**

I don't know if I have a good answer for this. That's just who I am. I could quite simply say that I love beautiful things. They make me happy. And beauty is everywhere – some natural, like the velvety wings of a butterfly, or the melting brown eyes of my dog, or the breathtaking blue of Lake Louise, or the ruggedness and remoteness of the Himalayas; and some we create through our muse – the turn of phrase, the well-knit story, the imagery, the cadence of rich text, the exhilarating screenplay, the amazing lighting, the perfect cameo, the sculptures, architecture, photographs, paintings, and so on. The list is as endless as the beauty and wonder of life around us.

17. **If there was someone in your past that could see what you are accomplishing now, and could give you some praise and/or feedback - which you valued above all else, who would that person be and why?**

My son passed away in 2013. His feedback was my gold standard - what I wrote, my acting, the productions as a whole...He was always spot on. His praise for something set the seal of success. He was one of the most creative people it has been my good fortune to know. His passing away leaves a gaping hole. My second son is also an artist. He is an actor, photographer, writer/director, but as he too relied on his brother's feedback and valued it at every stage, we are both feeling the loss immensely, as you can imagine.

18. **Do you ever co-write anything? If the first answer was "yes", then, what is important to consider before deciding to co-write anything with another author?**

I have co-written, and as a work that was produced, it has been successful. In any relationship, one leads. Which means the other should be comfortable with being second lead. They of course need to be 'on the same page' as regards subject, style, etc. Mutual respect and trust is important. Each one has to be genuinely convinced that each of them is great, but together they are greater. Where you want the work to go after it is completed, is another aspect where agreement is very important. This discussion should take place before the project begins, and it's best to embody it in an agreement along with leaving room for changes and what ifs.

**Thank you for taking the time to answer these questions, Jasmine.**

# *Ian*

**Ian's Story**

Why do I write?

It could be that it's easier than digging ditches. I know it's less strenuous than laying concrete blocks and since I don't like heights, roofing is out.

Maybe I write because it brings me pleasure telling an old acquaintance I write books and watch a look of disbelief cross their face. You know they're thinking 'you? Write a book? You've got to be kidding.'

A woman I knew asked if my first novel was based on a true story because she knew I couldn't have made it all up on my own. Now that's a true compliment.

I've never asked myself why I write or why I breathe or why I laugh at Monty Python. These are things I just do and one should not over-analyze what comes naturally, it might screw things up.

# The Dead Dog Van

Back in the seventies while still young and silly, I purchased a work vehicle from the Hamilton Humane Society. It was a tired old cargo van wearing several hundred thousand miles and if not for me, would have gone directly to the scrap heap, where my wife felt it belonged.

Before handing it over Society staff painted over their logos on both sides and the back and removed their large flashing light from the roof. The paint used did little to hide the blue HSPCA lettering so in the end, it still looked like a dead dog van.

Although it ran moderately well, I had to keep a case of oil and a small set of tools in the back to ensure I could get home whenever I ventured out on the road. The two seats up front were beat up and rickety, the radio never worked, and being an old empty van with numerous rattles, sounds tended to echo about its open interior making aspirin almost as important as the case of oil. My wife never became a fan of the old beast but I liked it and grew to enjoy scampering around Hamilton in my rather unique 'Dead Dog Van".

My two children also enjoyed it because they considered any trip with me an adventure and they got to sit on old wooden pop cases strewn about the back. Of course, this was an era when governments hadn't started caring for my children or me for that matter, and there were no seat belts, air bags or children's car seats fastened in an appropriate manner to government approved anchors. The cases worked fine until I purchased for five dollars the rear seat from a junk Ford Fairlane and bolted it to the floor. My son and daughter thought they were riding in luxury from that moment on.

Chewing gum was another thing my kids loved about the old van because when in it, they were allowed to chew multiple sticks to their heart's content. This was necessary because when it rained they had to take their gum and stick it in the holes in the ceiling left when the humane Society removed their light. We learned

---

this the first time it rained. It's quite surprising how much water can come through three half inch holes when you're doing fifty miles an hour. After that flood, the gum became as much a necessity as the aspirins and the oil.

During that time I was an elected member of Hamilton's city council representing Ward Six, an upper middle class to wealthy section of the east mountain. On occasion, when my wife had our car, I would use the van for transportation to my office at City Hall where one of the perks of the job was reserved parking for councillors. Almost every time I parked there at least one person would go into the City Clerk's office to report a strange looking vehicle sitting in the councillor's parking area. I think Ed Simpson and his staff grew a little tired explaining that the 'Dead Dog Van' in the Council Members Only parking area actually belonged to a council member.

I had that old van for about three years and when it finally died I felt kind of bad. It had served me faithfully and provided the family with a lot of laughs. It was also instrumental in keeping the motor oil and chewing gum industries strong and solvent. It did cause considerable comment about the City Council member who drove an old beat up Dead Dog Van but it never seemed to affect my ability to get re-elected. Somehow I don't think I could do the same these days.

I guess times have changed but I'm not sure if it's for the better.

# *Jasmine*

## Jasmine's Story

I just write. I love to read and so I love to write. I haven't really thought about the 'why' of it. When I feel very strongly about something, I don't speak; I write. Situations come to me, and the characters just appear in my mind. Dialogue begins, and soon I am writing it all down.

I guess I write because I want to be 'heard'. I was always discouraged from speaking – mostly by the nuns in school, with their 'silence is golden' rule. Writing is my way of speaking. Spoken words, once released, are a spent force, in the days when we had no easy access to recording.

But written words live on, if not forever, at least for a very long time, and are always there to go back to and savour.

# Saree Kahaniyan
## Saree Stories – One act play by Jasmine Sawant

**A tribute to sarees – that six yards of crisp cotton or shimmering silk, in hues and shades to match every mood, every moment, every journey of an Indian woman!**
**(Sarees are mostly worn by women in India and of Indian origin in the diaspora)**

## Present Day - Older JAG - Mississauga, ON, Canada

*(Dark. Sound of an old-fashioned clock ticking. Gradually brightening to reveal, an older woman, JAG, wearing a white saree with a beautiful border. She is in a dimly-lit room, sitting in an armchair, upstage right, napping. To her left, upstage centre, is a beat-up looking table, on which rests an old-style suitcase. Beside that are some books. The clock keeps ticking for a bit, and when it stops ticking, she wakes up with a start, mumbling).*

**Older JAG**: Oh dear, what time is it? Did I doze off? In this country many are the days when you can't tell whether it's night or day. And there are no clocks now, *(under her breath)* though, I thought I heard one. *(Then gives herself a shake and continues)*; only cell phones, and microwaves and TV black boxes to tell the time. None of which are present in this room, of course! And their thin, digital lettering, glowing eerily; it's useless! Sometimes, I can't even tell the time with my glasses on. *(Pause)* My glasses!!! Where are my glasses? Oh, here they are. Now let me go find out the time…. *(She rises painfully, as her knees hurt, shuffles a bit forward, and then decides to sit down)*. Well, what's the use? I am not hungry, so it's not mealtime. And there's nowhere to go. I'm not allowed to drive. Now, tell me, how do a few scratches matter? A Mercedes is still a Mercedes! But no, my son, the great Dharmaraj (Righteous One)! He thinks it's his civic duty to stop me from driving. *(Despondently)* No one has time for me, and I, have all the time in the world! So how does it matter, what time it is, or what day it is, or, what festival it is. Holi (Festival of Colours to welcome Spring) or Diwali (Festival of Lights to celebrate victory of good over evil) it's all the same. I am always wearing this white saree. Sure, the border is a different colour, (*with a chuckle*) it helps to know I am not wearing the same saree every day. And there's really no one to cook for. I can't eat half the stuff – high blood pressure, diabetes, or whatever they choose to call it, to stop me from eating all the *mithai* (Indian sweets). Gone are the days when every day, two questions were of utmost importance in my life – What to cook and what to wear? How times change - no husband, busy children, even busier grandchildren, it's just me in this little room, no, no, not 'little' it's a cosy room. That's the Canadian way to talk about it. (*Imitating her personal support worker*), "Oh my, Mrs. Swani, what a charmingly cozy room you have. Lovely books, (*under her breath*) which I can hardly read, (*continuing*) antique furniture, this vintage bag....!" My bag – my bag of life! (*Shuffles slowly to the suitcase*).

**Older JAG**: My sarees! They were my life! No, they are my life! A lifetime of memories, all here in this bag of sarees! (*Opens the suitcase, pulls out a saree and holds it close to her face.*) This was the first saree my husband bought for me. Don't remember where he bought it, or why. Looks a lot like a Bombay Dyeing (Indian manufacturer of bed and bath linens, etc.) curtain, but I was overjoyed. This was something **he** had selected for me, not his mother, or aunt or grandmother. Definitely not my style, but I got heaps of compliments whenever I wore it.

These flat folded materials may not look like much, but six yards of fabric, when wrapped around, pleated and tucked in, makes one look like a Goddess, so beautiful and elegant! How I loved my sarees! The colours, the textures, the weaves! And how I loved going saree shopping!!! Those were the days...ah... (*Sighs. Lights fade on older JAG and go up on the next scene that takes place downstage - A saree seller and a younger Jag in Mumbai. A noisy, crowded street, lined with saree shops on either side, a couple of jewellery shops, and other shops. The clientele is mostly women. The saree salespersons are mostly men*).

**The Saree Shop**

**Saree Seller (SS):** (*From the doorway of the store*) Welcome, sister (Vendors address potential women customers thus; meant to show respect), welcome! Buy sarees? For wedding?

**Jag**: No.

**SS**: For puja (Religious ceremony), party, mundan (A Hindu baby's tonsure ceremony), gift to mother-in-law, no problem, we have all latest styles.

**Jag**: No, no, I'm not buying.

**SS**: No problem, sister, come in, sister, only see, okay, no money to see.

(*Jag stops resisting and goes in*)

**SS**: Sit down, sister. (*To his young helper*) Ay (Commonly used to get someone's attention) chotu (Literally means little one; used to address a very young apprentice), A/C (Air conditioner) on kar (Switch it on). (*Back to Jag*) What will you drink sister? Chai (Tea), coffee, Thums Up (Brand of cola in India)?

**Jag**: Nothing, I only want to see some sarees.

**SS**: No problem, sister, all latest styles here. What range, sister?

**Jag**: About 2,000 rupees.

**SS**: What, sister, you from US, sister, increase budget, sister. What you get for 2,000 rupees?

**Jag**: Not the USA, I am from Canada, it's not the same country, you know.

**SS**: Arey (Commonly used exclamatory word), all dollars no, sister, then all same same. No problem.

**Jag**: Okay, okay, fine, show me in the range of 4,000 rupees.

**SS**: Okay, sister, all colours are okay, sister?

**Jag**: Yes, all colours, but no black.

(*SS starts showing various sarees, Jag keeps saying 'no', but soon she asks him to put aside a few sarees, as she wants to make up her mind later. Enter Other Customer (OC), who sits down beside Jag and slowly pulls out sarees from the heap in front of Jag. Neither Jag, nor SS pay her any attention. She keeps doing this, slowly, while waiting for the salesperson to attend to her.*)

**SS**: Okay, now I know your choice, sister. I show something exclusive, you will definitely like it, sister. See sister, your style, sober, but what get-up! Banarasi <sup>(From the city of Banaras in India)</sup> silk with Warli <sup>(Tribe living around the Gujarat-Maharashtra border. Their art/design ongoing since 3,000 BCE)</sup> design. All handwork, sister.

**Jag**: Yes, yes, it's good, but how much?

**SS**: Only 25,000 rupees, sister!

**Jag**: What! That's too much.

**SS**: What you saying, sister, Banarasi silk, all handwork. Seven karigars <sup>(Workers)</sup>, sister, took one month to make!!!

**Jag**: Okay, put it aside, let me think about it.

**SS**: Okay, sister, now have chai, sister?

**Jag**: No chai.

**SS**: Coffee, okay sister. (*To his young helper*) Ay chotu, ek <sup>(One)</sup> coffee, jaldi <sup>(Quickly)</sup>. (*To Jag*) Now I show you party sarees, sister.

**Jag**: No, no, enough!

**SS**: Sister, you select only five sarees. All classic style. Need party sarees also, no, sister. Lots of parties in US.

**Jag**: Canada, not the USA. And I am not buying, I am just looking. I still haven't decided.

**SS**: No problem, sister, no problem. See party sarees now.

(*Proceeds to show party-wear sarees. Jag has been eyeing the Warli saree, and sees it slowly sliding towards OC. She realizes that OC is taking it away and protests.*)

**Jag**: Excuse me! This is mine!

**OC**: Arey, it's just lying here, it's not yours! You haven't bought it.

**Jag**: No, I selected it, it's mine.

**OC**: You didn't. It's just lying here.

**Jag**: I did, it's mine. (*Turns to the SS*) You know it's mine.....
(*SS has moved away for a reason. Jag turning back to the OC*) Really! You have no courtesy, no manners. This is mine!

**OC**: No, it's not. And don't try to teach me manners. You rude lady!

**Jag**: You are snatching what's not yours, and calling me rude. Ulta chor kotwaal ko daatay (Pot calling the kettle black)! This is mine!

**OC**: You calling me a thief!

**Jag**: No, but you are behaving like one.

**OC**: Oye (Hey), phoren (foreign) lady, how you dare insult me. What you think of yourself, huh?

**Jag**: Now this is getting ridiculous! This **is** mine!

**OC**: Oye, NRI <sup>(Non-Resident Indian)</sup>, here take, take, don't want this stupid saree!!!

*(At this point, Jag wins the tug of war, because the Other Customer is distracted by another amazing saree)*

**Jag**: Mine!!! (*Lights fade and go up on Older JAG*)

## Back to Present Day

**Older JAG**: Mine!! Hahahah! What a victory! It wasn't very pleasant, arguing with her, but the saree was so worth it. Imagine! This is one of a kind. Unique! Makes me feel special each time I wear it. I have treasured each and every saree of mine, especially the very precious, very unique brocades, tanchois, ghajji silks, patolas <sup>(Different weaves)</sup>, handed down to me from my mother. (*Pointing to another pile of sarees*) And these are so beautiful even today. My grandmother had given these to my mother. (*Then she picks up a photograph and pointing to the saree in the picture*) This one, was such an exquisite saree, and it's gone! Hard to believe, but after that fateful day in Mumbai…when I lost this saree, even the thought of wearing a saree used to make me shudder. (*Lights fade on older JAG and go up on the next scene downstage.*)

## The Terrorist Attack

**Jag**: So, finally, how much did you put in the envelope?

**Navin**: I put… (*stops walking, pats his various pockets, with a horrified look on his face*).. I think… I think I left it on the… (*starts smiling*) you picked it up, didn't you? You have the envelope!

**Jag**: (*smiling*) Yes.

*(Navin shakes his head, smiles, and the two of them enter the Crystal Room, at The Taj Mahal Hotel Mumbai. Jag and Navin*

*go up to the married couple, smiling, greeting, shaking hands/doing Namaste* (Respectful greeting consisting of joining palms in front of oneself accompanied by the spoken word) *along the way. Going up to the newly wedded couple, they smile, congratulate, pose for pictures, etc.*)

**Jag**: Congratulations, Radhika, you are looking gorgeous!

**Navin**: Best wishes for a happy married life!

(*Suddenly loud sounds (gunshots) are heard in addition to the chatter of the guests, the clink of glasses and the wedding music. Jag looks worriedly at Navin*)

**Jag:** Are they gunshots!!! Here?!?

**Navin**: Must be drug lords duking it out in the back streets. Lately, rival gangs have become very active around the Gateway of India and this hotel.

**Jag**: I thought the hotel was sound proof. I can't understand why the police can't control them. This is such a high density tourist area! It should be safe at all times.

(*They begin to move to another part of the room to greet other people. Suddenly music stops and a hotel employee comes running in.*)

**Taj Employee** (TE): Ladies and Gentlemen, there is no cause for panic, but there's a bit of a situation here. For your safety, please maintain complete silence, and you will have to wait in darkness. We are about to switch off the lights. (*TE runs off. The sound of gunshots gets louder. They sound like the AK-47. They sound louder now. Very close. Everyone is very still, hearts beating with fear. Shots are fired into the room. Suddenly there's screaming and shouting. Jag and Navin run around in panic, with Jag tripping over her saree and almost falling a few times, bumping into stuff, and the saree getting caught in furniture that she can't see. Jag starts to fall and Navin bends to stop her from falling. At that very moment shots are fired again into the room. More screaming and shouting.*)

**Navin:** (*screeching*) Ooof! Oh my God! That almost got me!

(*Navin and Jag feel their way around to another part of the room. Gunfire again. Loud. They crawl under a table. Sounds of sporadic gunfire still heard in the distance – not as loud now.*)

**Navin**: Sitting here doing nothing is going to kill us. Let's try and get out of here!

**Jag:** God knows what the hotel is doing about this. Can't **we** call the police? Is it 911 here? Oh God! I can't remember! What is the emergency number here?

**Navin**: Damn! Can't remember! (*under his* breath) What is it? What is it? (*continues*) Got it! I think it's 100. (*Tries the number*). Busy!!! (*angrily*) How can an emergency number be busy? (*Keeps trying the number frustrated and also keeps shouting 'hello' 'hello'. With the light from the cell phones, they see people lying around wounded, bleeding, their breathing laboured, their hearts pounding with fear.*)

**Jag**: Oh God! (*crying*) These people are bleeding to death! Doctor! Is there a doctor here? (*no response*) Oh God! (*starts ripping her saree and trying to bandage a critically wounded person, whose guts have spilled out. After what seems like weeks, but was only thirty-six hours later, Navin and Jag struggle to their feet, exhausted, as rescue teams enter. They soon step out into the open, and look around at the chaos, and the unforgettable sight of the iconic Taj Mahal Hotel of Mumbai burnt! Jag is aghast at that sight, and then she glances down at her saree and is shocked – it's tattered and bloodied*)

**Jag**: Oh dear God! No! No! No! (*Stares at the hotel and down at herself, keeps crying and holding Navin's hand and leaning on him for support, walks off, refusing to talk to any of the media people who are out in large numbers, covering the terrorist attack. Navin also refuses to talk to the media, and holding Jag protectively by his side, walks away.*)

## Back to Present Day

**Older JAG:** That I lived to see such a day! So many dead! So much blood! My favourite hotel in flames! Mumbai attacked! Unthinkable, but it happened! And I stopped wearing sarees! Unthinkable, but that too, happened!

Each time I tried to wear a saree, all I could see was the blood-soaked fabric, and smell the sickening smell of human flesh and blood, and relive the terror. I didn't wear a saree for a very, very long time. Never thought there would be such a day!!! I was glad though, that my saree played such an important role. Had I not tripped when the pallu <sup>(The outer end of the saree that is more embellished)</sup> got caught, and had Navin not bent down to help me... (*in a whisper*)...we would have died that day. I was also glad that my saree became a useful piece of fabric to bandage that wounded man! But for a long time, I couldn't bring myself to wear a saree.

And then.....soon I was planning a wedding. My one and only daughter's wedding! How could I not go saree shopping? How could I not wear sarees for all those events – the mehendi <sup>(Henna ceremony)</sup>, the religious ceremonies, the reception, the puja...I went back to Bombay to shop for her wedding. How exciting it was! How delightful, but oh, how tired I used to get going from store to store, from Malad to Churchgate <sup>(Train stops on the Western Railway, Malad being in North Bombay and Churchgate in South Bombay)</sup>, buying sarees for her, for her in-laws to be, for our relatives, and of course for me! I literally bought hundreds of sarees, but the most memorable find was **that** saree, well almost like **that** saree. That saree that I had adored as a little girl, and then lost it forever, because I was being very stubborn, as only little girls can be. I can still remember that day......

## Loss of the *chundadi* <sup>(A special saree wore by a Hindu bride on her wedding day)</sup>

(*Little Jag clumsily draping the saree, and trying to apply lipstick, etc. She jumps, a bit startled, when she hears her mother's voice*).

**Mom**: Jagu, come finish your homework. (*No response*). Jagu!

**Jag**: Yes, mummy.

**Mom**: Come here at once. Finish your homework.

**Jag**: See, mummy, how do I look? (*Jag has her mother's wedding saree all incorrectly wrapped around her*)

**Mom**: Put that saree away, Jagu. Finish your homework.

**Jag**: But, tell me how I look, mummy, do I look like a bride?

**Mom**: (*Laughing*) Your wedding is still a long, long way off. Come now, finish this.

**Jag**: I want to look like you mummy, in your wedding saree. Tell me no, do I look like you? Do I look like a bride?

**Mom**: If you don't study well, no one will marry you, then you can't be a bride. Put that saree away and finish your homework!

**Jag**: Daadi says if I don't learn to cook, no one will marry me.

**Mom**: Jagu, you are not listening. Stop this nonsense right now! Finish your homework!

**Jag**: No, tell me, mummy, tell me, tell me, tell me.

**Mom**: You're trying my patience now, Jagu. You are not being good.

**Jag**: (*ignoring her mom, she goes round, chanting*) I look like a bride, I look like mummy, I look like a bride, I look...

(*At this point, Mom comes up close to Jag and slaps her.*)

**Mom**: That will teach you! You disobedient girl!

---

**Jag**: (*gasps, rubs her cheek, starts crying. Mom starts pulling off the saree.*)

**Jag**: (*between sobs begs her mother*) Mummy, don't mummy, I'll be good, don't mummy, I'll be good. Sorry, mummy, I'll be good.

(*Mom pulls the saree off her, turning her round and round to get the saree off. Mom then tosses the saree away. Unfortunately it goes out the window.*)

**Jag**: (*screams*) No, mummy don't throw it, mummy, I'll be good. (*She hangs on to her mother, who disengages her and leaves*).

(*Jag runs out to retrieve the saree, but can't find it anywhere, except for one little piece. She slowly comes back into the house holding it close and crying.*)

## Back to Present Day

**Older JAG:** Dear God. Now I am feeling miserable. How stupid the whole thing was. And to think it was my fault. That's what makes it so difficult. Finally, after all those years, I was so happy when I found a saree that was so similar to what my mother had worn on her wedding day. Ah here it is! This is what I wore at my daughter's wedding. (*Takes it out and lovingly touches it and puts it back*). So many sarees, so many stories! (*Rummaging through the bag and pulling a saree out, talking to herself, and putting it back*) This is the one he got for me when he went to Switzerland for the first time. It was a business trip, so unfortunately I couldn't go. But that's when he got me my first American Georgette saree. Ah! Here it is! It was very plain, so I had it embroidered. Now where is that one. Here! This one, the most treasured of all. There is such an enchanting story to it. It is what I call my 'kismet' kahani (Story) saree.

This is about the time when it was Bombay! Yes, Bombay, not

Mumbai. That time of my life, when 'bunking' college was an exciting thing to do, and that time in the history of Bombay when anything that was 'in town', meaning Fort Area, Colaba, Churchgate, was extremely exciting to me, the wide-eyed girl from the Northern suburbs.

## The First Meeting

### SCENE 1

**Ajay**: Hey Jag, let's go.

**Jag**: Ajiiiiiiiit! You're here! Thought you were in Dadar (A densely populated suburb of Bombay).

**Ajay**: How can I be in Dadar when I am here?

**Jag**: Shut up! Why aren't you in your techie class? You line 'marawing' (Trying to score with the girls) the girls or what?

**Ajay**: Girls! In engineering? Are you on 'charas (form of cannabis) or what? Ms. Charsee Monjee!

**Jag**: Shut up! It's Narsee Monjee College.

**Ajay**: Never mind! Let's go.

**Jag**: Where?

**Ajay**: To town

**Jag**: Yay!!! But why?

**Ajay**: To see a film.

**Jag**: Where?

**Ajay**: Regal.

**Jag**: Why Regal? Why not Eros?

**Ajay**: How does it matter, It's an English film, that's all.

**Jag**: Liar! I know why Regal! You want to go to Elphie to meet Anju.

**Ajay**: Not meet her, pick her up. She's coming with us to the movie.

**Jag**: Hahahah. Clever with words, aren't you? If Anju and you, are going, why do you need me? Kabaab mein haddi (Two is company, three is a crowd)!!! Why? Why?

**Ajay**: Come on. You know why. She can't come out with me otherwise.

**Jag**: Hahahah! Of course, I knew that.

**Ajay**: Don't waste time! Let's go.

**Jag**: Hold on, hold on. I have to attend the next lecture. It's a very important. Statistical Analysis.

**Ajay**: Forget it! If I can bunk engineering, why can't you bunk your silly commerce stuff.

**Jag**: It's not silly. And you are in 'luuv'. I am not.

**Ajay**: Oh, Come on!

## SCENE 2

(*They walk into Elphinstone College*)

**Jag**: Ajay, wait, what if they ask us for ID?

**Ajay**: They won't.

**Jag**: Oye, Mr. Know-it-All. How do you know they won't. (*Then without waiting for Ajay's reply, Jag just stops walking and starts looking around. This is the first time she's visited Elphinstone College and she's busy admiring the architecture and reading the plaques on the wall.*)

**Jag**: Oh my God! This is so beautiful! Ajay look at this! It's real stone! Oh my God! It is..no..yes..Yes!!! It's Gothic…

**Ajay**: Gothic, shothic, big deal, let's go get Anju.

**Jag**: No…maybe…. I had no idea Elphinstone College was that old!!!

(*Ignoring Ajay, Jag looks all around, then glances up above the entrance through which they had just entered and starts speaking to herself.*)

**Jag**: Past Principals. 1845! 1862! (*Lets out a big scream*) Oh my God! Oh my God! Oh my God! 1874! William Wordsworth. Can you believe it! William Wordsworth was principal here! He walked through these very doors that I just walked through. He went up these very stairs….composing….imagine composing "Daffodils", here!!! (*Bursts into poetry*) I wandered as lonely as a cloud that floats on high o'er vales and hills, when all at once I saw a crowd, a host of golden daffodils. Beside the lake, beneath the trees, fluttering and dancing in the breeze…..

**Ajay**: Have you ever seen daffodils grow in Bombay!! William couldn't have composed it here. Moreover (*pause*) William Wordsworth died in 1850. Come on, silly!

**Jag**: But…but…the list says…

**Ajay**: No, buts, come on now!

**Jag**: Okay, Mr. Know-it-All!

(*They go up the stairs, down the corridor, and standing in the doorway of a class that is still on, Ajay works at getting Anju out of her class.*)

**Ajay**: 'Pssst' 'Shhhh', Anju. (*Anju comes out*)

**Anju**: Ajay, what are you doing here?!?

**Ajay**: Movie, come on, it's getting late. This silly Jag was busy reciting poetry, otherwise…

**Anju**: (*cuts in*) I can't. I have lab work.

**Ajay**: What the heck? You promised.

**Anju**: Yes, but, I can't, not today…please… (*Bell rings. Class ends and out comes Venkie*)

**Venkie**: Thanks, Anju, thanks. That's brilliant!

**Anju**: (*confused*) What did I do?

**Venkie**: Thanks for getting me into trouble.

**Anju**: Arey! Say hello to Ajay and Jag first.

**Venkie**: Sorry. Hi! Ajay, Jag. Thanks, ya, Anju, thanks.

**Anju**: Don't get dramatic, you idiot! What happened?

**Venkie**: Rollcall. I didn't see you in class, so when the Prof called out your name, I said "present, sir". But he saw you leave class. Dash it. Why didn't I see him seeing you leave? I wouldn't have proxied for you!

**Anju**: (*laughing*) Stupid! You shouldn't have. Why did you?

(*Venkie's anguished face was so comical that Anju, Ajay and Jag burst out laughing loudly.*)

**Venkie**: Thanks, thanks, keep laughing. Sheesh, friends! Who needs them. Bye, I got to go for extra tutorials now. Thanks to you!

## SCENE 3

*(The next day.)*

**Jag:** Hi Girish!

**Girish**: (*a serious, hard-working student, all set to get his C. A. credentials*) Jag, where were you yesterday? I didn't see you in Stats class. It was a very important lecture. How could you miss it?

**Jag**: Never mind Stats. Guess what happened yesterday! I went to town with Ajay. We went to Elphinstone College to pick up Anju and watch a film.

**Girish**: You went all the way to Elphie! If I had known, I would have come with you. I have a friend there!

**Jag**: You wouldn't have bunked Stats, though. Anyway, listen, na! Then there was this guy who proxied for Anju, but the Prof had seen her leave, and so this guy got into trouble. He got extra tutorials for trying to proxy! (*laughs heartily*)

**Girish**: (*Laughing*) Sounds like my friend. Just the kind of thing he would do. What was this guy's name?

**Jag**: Umm…hold on…it's coming to me…Navin Savani!

**Girish**: Oh Fish! That **is** my friend. (*Laughs again*) Imagine you meeting him like that!!! I should have been there!

**Jag**: (*More laughter*) He was so upset with Anju. It was so funny. (*Both laugh*)

**Girish**: I'm meeting him tomorrow at Khar Gymkhana. Why

don't you come? We'll pull his leg some more.

**Jag**: Sure. That will be fun! I will be there.


## SCENE 4

(*The next day.*)

**Mom**: Jagu, where are you going?

**Jag**: To meet some friends.

**Mom**: Dressed like that!

**Jag**: What's wrong with this dress? It's in fashion.

**Mom**: Really Jagu. Wearing such itsy bitsy pieces of fabric is not called dressing, it's undressing!

**Jag**: Really Mom! Not again! Minis are in fashion. Stop being so old fashioned.

**Mom**: Fashion is for film stars, child. People from good homes dress decently. It's high time you started wearing a saree. Soon you will be married.

**Jag**: Precisely. Once I get married I will be wearing sarees all my life! Let me wear what I want now.

**Mom**: How you've changed. When you were younger, you kept wrapping yourself up in my sarees. You refused to change into a dress, even though you kept tripping up. (*Annoyed*) Now look at you! (*suddenly cajoling*) Come on, now Jagu. Be sensible. What will the neighbours say, if you go out in this!

**Jag**: I don't care, and you shouldn't either.

**Mom**: (*getting more and more upset*) Jagu, I wish you cared.

When you go out dressed like that, it reflects on me. Then everyone says I don't know how to raise my daughter properly. And your grandmother starts her lecture, then she complains to your Dad, and then he…and then he…

**Jag**: (*cutting in*) Okay, Mom, please no histrionics! For you, I will wear a saree, okay. Now cheer up! Which one should I wear?

*Mom*: (*cheering up*). How about this one?

**Jag**: (*rolling her eyes*) Maroon. Too fancy! (*sees her Mom looking a bit down again, and gives in*) OKAY, fine. Whatever you want, now cheer up.

**Mom**: (*As Jag is leaving in a saree*) You look so lovely! (*sighs*)

**Jag**: (*hugging her mom*) Bye, Ma. Be good. (*winks and is out the door.*)

## SCENE 5

**Jag**: Hi Girish, hope I am not late!

**Girish**: No, you're unfashionably early. (*He smiles, Jag makes a face*) Saree and all, oooh!!! Who you trying to impress???

**Jag**: Shut up! Where's your friend?

**Girish**: (*turning towards Navin*) Once again, meet my friend, Navin Savani. (*Starts laughing*)

(*Navin stands up. Both Navin and Jag keep looking at each other, Jag extends her hand to shake. Navin unfolds his arms and extends his hand. They look at each other but don't shake hands.*)

**Back to Present Day**

**Older JAG**: That was how I met my husband, for the very first time. Yes, it was the very first time. Girish kept laughing and never realized that we had never met before. In those days, I never forgot names and faces, but strangely, that day, when Girish asked me the name of that poor proxy fellow, the incorrect name just popped into my head. Navin Savani! Just like that, out of nowhere. Had I read, or heard of this name before, I could have understood why it popped, but I never had. Nobody in my family had known anyone by that name. It was truly destiny! We were meant to meet and marry. Some years later I asked my husband, why he hadn't said anything that day to clear the confusion. With a big smile he gently said, "My dear, do you think I am stupid? How could I tell a beautiful girl that I don't know her? And then, I was so mesmerized by this lovely vision in a red saree. At that moment, I couldn't even remember my own name!"

My maroon saree, not red, maroon, but men and colours... My most favourite one of all. A bit faded now... like me, I suppose. (*Older Jag wraps the saree, around her, shuffles to downstage centre, as though preening herself in the saree*) (*Fade out*)

## THE END

All stories are based on real life events and experiences

# *John*

## John's Story

John writes motivational articles and poetry exploring life's triumphs. He writes from a desire to express emotions, encourage, stimulate, motivate and have fun.

He enjoys moving from writing's creative solitude to connecting with an audience on deeper levels. Uncovering where his writing journey leads, the people, learning's, and places along the way is a constant evolution.

# Torn Pages

It lay there, a crumpled heap
A Torn Page, no one would weep
It lay there, a vivid reminder
Of ideas, emotion, dreams, thoughts, caught in failures' binder

A Torn Page, there were so many
Of chapters started, and verses plenty
Thoughts would come, ideas would go
Another Torn Page, amidst the throw

Could s/he write? Could s/he start again? Could s/he heal?
The Torn pages beckoned, but rarely when
Could s/he dream? Could s/he love?
A torn page, was there no God above?

Despair is not written on the torn page
Despair is torn from hearts full of rage
For torn pages are but one of many crumpled dreams
Not wasted effort, but steps towards life's greater theme

No book, no life, no dream was ever written
Without a torn page, within its seams
Fruit's taste is released by piercing its skin
A shell is torn, not the vitality within

From every torn page, a library is born
Resources for life, to heal the forlorn
So do not regret the torn pages that lie
Truth is found in brighter skies

Fabric is formed from many fibres
Resiliency darts within the shadows of power
Who really knows if a page is truly torn?
Or just the spark of a new life form!

# Remember to Look UP!

Remember to look UP....
From your devices (TV, iPhone, BB, stellar-link*to be invented)
Into the faces of those you love.

Remember to look UP....
Text can only generate a smile
When we've looked up to see one.

Remember to look Up....
To see the direction you are travelling
Rushing often moves backwards as much as forwards.

Remember to look Up....
Blue Sky is possibility thinking
Gratitude for how wondrous is the Universe!

Remember to look Up....
Into a friendly mirror
Reflecting only positive messages back.
It matters how you see yourself.

Remember to look UP....
Children need to see parents' smile
More than a video screen.

Remember to look UP....
For to look down on any other race or person
Means you have not looked up or in. (which looks down on
you).

Remember to look UP....
To see Her pain, His frustration
Everyone carries a story.

Remember to look UP
Connection is a key to resiliency

Did you make the world a better place, today?

Remember to look UP....
Choice, awareness and blessing
It takes so little to improve someone else's day,
Including your own.

Remember to look UP....

# Have you ever had a bad day?

Have you ever had a bad day?
One where all of life appeared to go astray?
Crisis, despair, anger, frustration, depression, lost,
Anxious, energy wasted and at what cost?
Have you ever had a bad day?

Have you ever had a bad day?
Train was late, now so am I
Flustered, frustration accelerates confusion
Took 10 minutes to find my keys in this mess
Phone call, crisis, unexpected delay
I really should have left much earlier today
Have you ever had a bad day?

Have you ever had a good day?
Wake up. It's all going to be just fine
Breathe. I'm alive. Grateful family and love is so close
I can even like myself the most
Not conceited, not brash, but humble and kind
Appreciating good feelings brings peace of mind
Balance, harmony, peaceful, bliss
If she were awake, oh my, what a kiss
Letting her sleep, treasuring her grace
Have you ever had a good day?
Where you're amazed how kids play and make games of fun
How does your good day begin and end?
Receptive good days, open mind, open heart, open to others,
judged not
Enjoying, calm, determined, move forward, actualizing,
Have you ever had a good day?

Have you ever had a good day?
Tolerant to differences,
No longer adhering just to right and wrong,
Courting justice more than a blaming lawyers song
Intrinsic wisdom, sees more than black and white
Perceives even the colours of the night

Course corrections are what society needs
More than the litany of government misdeeds
Understanding is born out of mutual respect
Awareness comes when we let go of regret
Have you ever had a good day?
Have you ever had a good day?

# SPACE

Space
It has been called: "The Final Frontier"**
Mankind's thirst for discovery
Is there life beyond?
Do we escape our madness
Only to destroy another planet beyond?

Space
What is the distance from earth to the moon?
Copernicus, Galileo,
From Milky Way to Sagittarius dwarf sphere
Ursa Major II to Large Magellanic Cloud
Where distance is measured in millions of light years

Columbus
What if he had never set sail?
One small step we map now from galaxy to galaxy
Gemini, Apollo, Saturn V and Soyuz
Travelling the heavens like an oceanic cruise

Earth
Do we see how fragile it is?
Will we be just a statistic in the Universe's quiz?
Water planet, a jewel, green this resource
Endangered species Man could one day be
So much for the Sea of Tranquility

Space
Protect it
Earth
Preserve it. Care for it.
Space, between you and me
Transverse it, with care
Space

** "Space: The Final Frontier" is the first line of the opening
voiceover in Star Trek read
by James Tiberius Kirk (Created by Gene Roddenberry).

# STOP

Stop. Stop and Go. Stop and Go.
Stuck in traffic. Too and frow.
Oh NO! I'm going to be late.
The pressure builds.

I cannot change, the cars ahead
Even with a foot of lead
I can change the thoughts in my head
No point speeding up my internal clock
This is just a time to stop.

Stop.
Stop and calm the rush inside.
Stop peacefully and be alive.
Stop and breathe. Relax your mind.
Stop. Why aggravate your beautiful mind?
Stop. What would happen if you were dead?
Stop. Anxiety kills many brain cells.
Stop. Relax. All is well.
Stop making a living hell.
Stop and smile. Leave earlier next time.
Stop. Enjoy the sun, cloud or even those painted yellow lines.
Stop. Four inches of paint on a highway and it keeps you alive.
Stop. Pay attention. The world did not end.
Stop. Enjoy, every moment my friend.
Stop. Renew your focus in calmness again.
Stop. Peace of mind. Be kind to your mind.
Stop. This moment will not come again.

Relax. Moving one step ahead
Calm. Take the next step, plan well my friend.
Go. Be ready and be prepared.
Go. No time to be scared.
Go. And Stop. Are you doing just fine?
Go and stop. What if this moment was all there is?
Make the most of it, instead of being in a fizz.
Go. Calmly. Peacefully. Kindly. Awake. Aware. Go steady.

Yes, I notice this is where I'm placing my keys.

---

Find them next time with much more ease.

## Your Mind Can Take You Places

Your mind can take you places
Many to where you don't want to go
Negative, dark, "you're stupid, you're off the mark"
"I can't, I blew it, I have to, and I'm trying"
Stop now.  Put on the brakes. Shift gears.

Take a moment. Breathe. Turn this around.
Captain of your ship, take gentle control at the helm.

Breathe. Breathe. Yes, it's easy as 1, 2, 3.
Reset your mind.  Breathe. Breathe with me.
Be your own best friend
Self-criticism or Self-praise
On which would you rather graze?
So begin, now. Take a moment, 1, 2, 3.
And B r e a t h e.
I am my own best friend.

I am.

Parts of your mind, may be in pain
So look at all the other parts that are free to play
Find them. Discover. To the left, to the right.
Up, or down. Over here, over there.
Somewhere inside your mind
It's safe, it's fun, it's kind, it's calm, it's peaceful,
It's positive. Yes, I am. Yes, I will spend more time there.

You have a gift. A talent. Many things you enjoy.
Your children. Your work. Finding a job if unemployed.
A friend to listen. A friend would listen.
So be a friend, my friend. Be your own best friend.

Joy. Wonder. Hope. Discovery. Creation. Health.
Good person. Good friend. Kind heart. Kind words.
I am capable. I am good. I am learning. I am.

Your mind can take you places you CAN
Go to the grocery store of goodness inside your mind
I can abundantly shop there for more than I know
Joy. Wonder. Hope. Discovery. Creation. Health.
These good products I can find on my shelf.
I can pick, I can, a can of Joy, I can accept all, that is inside
myself
Abundantly nurturing my gifts, for others to see.
I am alive. Moving from me to we.

# Intruder

Stillness now gripped the night
A creak, a click, a footstep?
Intruder?
Or just a tree branch tapping outside?

Stillness now gripped the night
What was that sound?
Above heartbeat's fright
Racing thoughts imagining danger near
All the product of unnecessary fear

Stillness now, the alarm has passed
No danger
At least that is what she thought
Her muscles shouldn't be this taught
No danger
The sound has passed
Silent stillness

Stillness now no need for fear
Danger is passed, no risk is near
Till click, the door, O God, someone is there
Creak, it opens, a footstep, methodically stops
Creak, the door, opens, another bump
Another footstep
Her throat now in a lump

Stillness now, her body rigid
Floorboards creak. Were keys left in the lock?
Intruder is real, foreboding shock
Intruder, steps, his breath is heard
Floorboards creak, a step
How to run and alert the kids
How to get out, is he armed?
The steps have opened another door

Stillness now, she must not be detected
She matches her steps to each floorboard creak
Her heart racing ever louder still
Wait, a light, the fridge, what thief stops for a meal?
Drunk again. "TOM! What the hell?"
Stillness now, in this house, a thing of the past
But will he think and remember before raising another glass?

# Pathways

A path in the woods
Quiet walk, nature understood
A path down a country road
Exploring adventure, unknown territory, foreign land
Mighty trees tower in the woods
Sunlight penetrates the canopy
Nature, creation, harmony, fragile balance
Marvel at the silence, from the dawn of time
Nature, solitude, universe, divine, purpose, align
Pathways in the mind unexplored
Photosynthesis
Two trees, air for one person
Pathways undisturbed
Moss, lichen, insects, birds, fruit, leaves,
Ecosystem decaying nutrients nourishing new growth
Pathway to respect
Pathway to next generation
Pathway to preservation
Pathway to life
Pathway to destruction if destroyed
Pathways lead
Pathways beckon
Pathways, fork in the road
Pathway to discoveries untold
Pathways calling us to be bold
Pathways' future unfold
Pathways' choice
Pathways of apathy or action
Pathways turn
Pathways change
Pathways' choice
Pathways
Environmental pathway protection a must
If the human species is not to return to the dust
From global collapse of nature's order

Nature itself knows no border
Chemicals in time creep and seep
DNA alteration, soil contamination, human degradation
Pathways misunderstood until it's too late
Science can save or destroy
Be careful which engineering you employ
Pathways to pause upon and reflect
Some pathways in the mind can be suspect
Pathways

# Cloudy Days

Cloudy Days blot out the sun
Yet Cloudy Days can be fun
Every pilot knows above the clouds to soar
Let me go there now, in my mind, lest I become a bore.

Cloudy Day
Clouds never block out the sun, only our view,
From where we are standing
Tomorrow, clouds will have moved on
Will you be standing in the same or different spot?
Clouds may cloud the mind
Clouds can give shade when in need
Clouds deliver rain's precious seed
Clouds bring both calm and storm
Clouds are always changing, don't live in the storm
Clouds give way to brighter skies
Blue Sky and clouds, part of earth's rotation
Without clouds, would we have vegetation?
Mysteries can be cloudy and dark
Mysteries bring discovery, excitement, when we embark
So do not fear a cloudy day
Be patient with life's season,
If just for a day
Live today
Clouds, clouds, go away
Come again another day
Rain or clouds, does it matter?
Enjoy the laughter
Rise above the clouds to where the sun always shines still
Pilot now, Captain of your soul
Break free from clouds
Or just wait, the clouds will clear
Clouds
Don't forget why you are here.
Clear?
Clear!

# Listening

Listening
It always is a matter of the heart
Don't wait, just pick a place to start
Children listen when we've heard them first
Understand and see what other's see
Make a change, from 'all about me'.

Listening
He listened
She heard my heart
Calm and reflective
Not pushing his own agenda
Time, it was unhurried
Space, comfortable and connected
Eyes, they met, soft and warm
Inviting, this moment was safe
This place was safe
She listened so well I sensed
She knew me better than myself
Or maybe it was just that I felt heard
Situation, feelings, no longer absurd
Listening
Listing, listing side to side, drowning
When the mind is too busy to calm down
Deafness to purpose is often found
So start listening more, face to face
Two ears, two eyes, two nostrils, one mouth
Ears to hear, eyes to see, nose to sense, and then I may speak
Two ears, two eyes, two nostrils, one mouth
God got the order right.
Listening to others, listening to oneself
Listen for God's still voice
Calm listening
Listen

# Memories

The apple pie cooling on the kitchen window
Mother's smile at baby's first glance
Little fingers, little hand, little toes, of a little man
Now he catches his very first ball
Giggles and delights, children do enthral
Each present moment is a future memory somewhere
Why do we live our lives, at times, so unaware?

Memories of her first skate
Memories of his first at bat
Memories of their first school test
Memories of grandpa coming, just to walk grandson to school
Memories of that teacher, who was mediocre at best
Memories of that teacher, who showed interest and more
Memories of kindergarten just begun
Memories move freely through time

High school's friends, what a diverse array
Mumbai, Texas, Toronto, Pakistan, Poland and China
Edmonton, Nova Scotia, 'yo brother wuts up?' This is Canada.
He shoots, he scores. Her salchow. Failed test. Excellent speech.
They took the provincial Championship. Too much to drink last
week.
Now off to University and baseball, even in the USA!
Admiring who they will become someday.

Memories of the wedding and the first dance.
Memories of first kiss, first night, first love, first insignificant
fight.
Memories of the hopes and dreams, and also life's circumstance.
Memories of vacations, beauty....................and
encountering sickness and death.
Memories of resilience and doing our best.
Memories of triumph, of closeness, of touch, of kindness, of
caring, of life.
Memories of friends, activities, and late evenings shared, of

parties and joy.
Memories of mountain tops and valleys traversed
Memories, without them, life would be worse.

Memories, what will our children remember?
Will it be of all the toys they got that December?
Or of how I spoke, of how I listened, of how I was there, of how I cared?
Of letting them grow, achieve, learn and recover, of being an open door.
Memories of Nativity, Divine spark.
Memories of family Christmas dinner, and 'twas the night before.
Memories are gifts, life's jewelled treasures, diamonds in our mind.
Memories. Treat them well.

# Seasons

On a cold winter's day
The sun did shine
Crisp snow. Frozen air
White powder blankets
On every tree
Branches bending beneath
Thousands of icy white sheaths
Winter's Wonderland.

Bare branch, a bud, a bud here, many buds there
Tiny tips of green silhouetted by the blue sky
Tiny tips of green pushing up from the ground
Tulips, daffodils, crocuses, hyacinth, magnolia, evergreen
Red, yellow, purple, blue, pink and green
Nature, Life, Mountains, Green grass, Lakes and streams
All wonders to be seen
Spring has sprung. Nature's smile. Joy in step.

Hot sun, warm air, massive green leaves
Held up in the air. Trees even give us the air we breathe
One tree, Oxygen for one, absorbs 48 lbs. $CO_2$/year
One acre of trees, eighteen people can breathe
Summer crops, Summer vacation, Summer BBQ. Summer fun
Fresh fruit, strawberries, peaches, berries, and wine
Summer lakes. Summer love. Summer Sun
Yellow, Green, Blue, Brown, Green, Red.

Large rolls of hay, Apples, Pumpkins, Turkey
Kaleidoscope of yellow, orange, red, brown, gold, and green
Cooler, leaves falling to the ground, shimmering shoreline
Ablaze of nature's artistic canvas
Nourishing the soil for spring
Dotting the landscape still piercing evergreens.

Seasons of colour. Is that why it snows?
Seasons change. Seasons grow.
Seasons do more than I know.
Seasons, how many seasons has this tree stood?

Seasons so I can enjoy my walk in the woods.
Seasons

# *Joseph*

## Joseph's Story

I began writing years ago when I wrote a letter to the editor of The Toronto Sun. The letter was a rebuttal to their editorial about Rock'N'Roll fans being too aggressive and violent. It was very gratifying when my letter got published.

**Later that year, the same** newspaper held a creative writing contest where I was one of the top 15 winners out of dozens of entries. This remains one of my greatest accomplishments.

What writing means to me is that it gives me an outlet to express my opinions. I grew up introverted and shy. Writing was, and still is, the best way I convey my feelings.

# The Torn Page

Ralph was sifting through his desk drawer. His original intention was to search for a pen. He discovered something he didn't anticipate on finding there. He found the torn page of a newspaper clipping. When he examined it, he saw listed lottery numbers from an earlier draw.

Upon further scrutiny, he saw something familiar with the numbers. They looked eerily similar to numbers he had played in the past. At this point, he decided to walk over to the drawer where he stores old lottery tickets.

To his delight, he finds one ticket that has the *exact* numbers that are listed on the newspaper page. He immediately fantasizes about how he can buy his dream car and his dream home. Soon he'll be booking his dream vacation!

How much has he won, he asks? The jackpot prize is listed as 10 Million dollars. He is frustrated, though. The torn page is ripped right where the date of the draw was printed. He thinks of a solution to his dilemma. He'll visit the Winning Lottery Numbers page of the National Lottery Corporation.

Ralph has mixed emotions. He is nervous; he is elated. Soon the moment of truth will be upon him. He scrolls down the page to check the winning numbers from the past 12 months. Low and behold, he spots the numbers that match up with the numbers on his ticket.

Now he is *really* nervous and excited! He carefully checks the date of the winning numbers. The date of the lottery draw of the winning numbers is November 1, 2013. At this point, he stops. He slowly turns his head to the calendar on the wall. The date circled is --gasp!--November 2, 2014. What a shocker: the date to collect his winnings has passed.

All his dreams are shattered. He *still* doesn't have the money to buy his dream car, house, or vacation. He falls back in his chair. How could he have been so careless? What a costly mistake, to say the least, it was not to check his ticket months earlier?

Beside him is a bottle of ant-acid tablets. If it was a bottle of cyanide, it would be more appropriate for the situation.

That torn page must be the most expensive in the history of mankind!

# Brigid II: The Transporting Device is Reinvented

## Part I: Frank Lyon Reinvents the Transporting Device

Frank Lyon is on his couch in front of his flat-screen T.V. on New Year's Eve of 2003. The channel is tuned in on Dick Clark's Rockin' New Year's Eve live from Time's Square in New York City.

The sight he is viewing on T.V. leaves an impression on him. That is because two short years earlier, he had been at that very sight ringing in the New Year of 2002.

He turns his head and glances at the picture of his late wife, Brigid. A tear trickles down his cheek, as he is disappointed by the fact she wasn't there to share the moment then or now. In spirit, he can hear her say, "Hey, Frankie, do you think we're the best looking couple at Time's Square tonight?!"

He can't help but chuckle when he replies, "Honey, we're always the best looking couple, no matter where we are!"

At this moment, the final countdown begins with the ball dropping down ushering in the New Year: '10, 9, 8, 7, 6, 5, 4, 3, 2, and 1...Happy New Year...! A hand is suddenly placed on his shoulders. It is his son, Jimmy, who passes his father a glass of champagne by saying [sounds awkward]: 'Here, Dad, let us toast to health and happiness in the year 2004."

Frank drinks the glass of champagne, rises from his chair, and hugs his son and says: "All the best to you, son, for the New Year, also." Frank Lyon once again hears Brigid talking from above: "These are two fine gentlemen I'm looking down on. Wish I was there!" Frank replies: "You are here in spirit, honey!"

Frank replies by saying: "To your departed mom, Jimmy, she's with us in spirit!"

Jimmy replies: "That she is.  Say "hello" to her for me."

Frank says: "That I will do!"

The New Year is barely half an hour old, and already CNN reports that there is the first murder of 2004.  Frank is disgusted with this news and turns the T.V. off.  He and Jimmy retire to the bedroom so that they will be prepared to watch the Rose Bowl parade and game later on in the morning.

It's 10:00 a.m. on New Year's Day.  Frank awakens before his son to a cold and snowy day in Readfield, Maine.  He decides to make a bacon and egg breakfast.  Afterwards, he sits in his comfortable chair and picks up the "TIME" magazine that is resting on the coffee table.  He reads the headline on one of the articles, when he flips the pages that read: "Airplane Jet Fuels Cause 40 % of Greenhouse Gas Emissions Every Year".  Frank is startled by that enormous percentage.  He continues reading the article and becomes even more flabbergasted by the disturbing facts about airplane exhaust fumes and how they damage the earth's atmosphere.  A few minutes later, Jimmy sits in the easy chair beside him.

Frank turns to Jimmy and says:  "There is an interesting article in this week's "TIME" magazine.  It points out how the earth's atmosphere is being considerably damaged by airplane exhaust fumes."

Jimmy, with an inquisitive look on his face, replies by saying: "How bad is the damage?"

It is at a point that Frank reiterates a paragraph from the article.  He reads it by saying:  *"Airplane exhaust fumes account for 40 % of the total Greenhouse Gas Emissions emitted into the earth's atmosphere.  Scientists conducting the study estimate that, at this rate, airplane exhaust fumes can easily become the primary source of Greenhouse Gas Emissions being dispersed into the earth's atmosphere within 5 years."*

Jimmy is startled by what he is hearing. "I don't want you to read anymore, dad! I am shocked that airplanes can do this much damage to the earth's atmosphere. If only we can do something to slow the rate by even 10%, I would do it today!"

Frank replied with a disappointed tone in his voice by saying: "We are just 2 people out of a few billion on earth. If we put our heads together, maybe we can find a way. After all, it's the little things that make a big difference!"

The grandfather clock on the wall chimed 11 times, indicating that it was 11 o'clock in the morning. Frank and Jimmy temporarily glanced to the T.V. set to continue watching the Rose Bowl Parade. As they were watching, Frank observed something interesting. On each float, several people were being transported from one place to another all at once. Frank has a "Eureka" moment! Just like the floats, airplanes transport people from one place to another. He links this idea with the concept of the transporting device. Could this be the beginning of something that could save the Earth's environment?

He turns to Jimmy and declares: "Jimmy; do you see what I see?"

Jimmy looks puzzled by saying: "Yeah – it's a bunch of happy people waving from floats in a parade, going from one point to another!"

Frank excitedly says, "You said the key words to saving the environment!"

Jimmy is very puzzled, turns to his dad and says: "What words have I just said that can save the earth's environment?"

Frank reiterates those words: "...a bunch of people...going from one point to another...!"

Jimmy doesn't understand at first what his dad is driving at; he replies to his dad, still puzzled: "All that these people are doing is celebrating a happy occasion: what's your point?"

Frank is exalted! He can now explain to Jimmy that he has found a solution to eliminating 40% of Greenhouse Gas Emissions. To clarify his solution, Frank continues bantering with Jimmy.

"Jimmy, what was so significant about the transporting device?"

Jimmy replied by saying: "You could get from one place to another without the aid of a vehicle of any sort."

Frank confirmed this by saying: "Precisely! I have come up with a way of doing that again!"

"What do you mean by 'again'?" replied Jimmy inquisitively.

Frank continued to explain: "Starting tomorrow, I am going to design a blueprint of a machine that can transport a plane-load of people from one location to another without flying in the air!"

Jimmy replied in a puzzled manner by saying: "The transporting device could only transport one person at a time. You are trying to tell me you can invent something that can transport many more people at once?"

At this point, Frank excitedly rises from his chair and exclaims: "You are damn right about that! It will no longer be a 'device'; it will be"—at this point he extends his arms about 4 feet apart-- ..."a machine!" He continues by saying: Two-thousand and four is going to be the year that Frank Lyon becomes TIME magazine's Person of the Year! I am jumping the gun a little bit, though!

Jimmy tells him: "You can say that again! I am wondering how I can help you with all this."

Frank reassures Jimmy by saying: "Now that you have graduated from College, you will be here in Readfield every step of the way."

The rest of New Year's Day is spent relaxing from all the excitement of the Rose Bowl game and post-New Year's Eve celebrations.

On the morning of January 2, 2004, Frank gets up and enthusiastically boots up his computer. He doesn't wake up his son yet, as he would like to design the Transporting Machine in a quiet environment and uninterrupted.

On his computer, he has a programme that can aid in the design of the 'transporting machine'. He needs to figure out some basic features of this machine. First, it will need to transport 200 people at once. Secondly, it will require an input feature that can activate it and get it from one place to another. Thirdly, it must contain sophisticated security features that must make it unable to be duplicated by any organization other than the one who operates it.

With these 3 criteria, Frank embarks on his new creation. He realizes that it will be several months in the making from design to construction. To him, it doesn't matter. Frank is very concerned about the environment; not only as a scientist, but as a caring human being. He will leave no stone unturned.

In the first hour, he has designed the dimensions of the Transporting Machine. It is 100 feet by 100 feet by 100 feet. Since transportation is instantaneous, passengers who use the machine will inhabit compartments standing up. The compartments will have enough space for 2 people. The compartments will be 75 cubic feet. Passengers will be buckled into gurney-like seats so that they will not be startled while transported. Each machine transports 200 people; therefore, there are 100 compartments in all in the transporting machine.

# *Kim*

# Kim's Story

Growing up as a child, I started writing in a diary. I found that there was never enough space in the preprinted diaries to get all my thoughts and feelings into them, so I began to use loose leaf paper and a binder to hold all my thoughts. I always felt like through writing I could describe the things around me, the situations that I encountered and my deepest feelings. I began writing poetry as a young teenager to deal with all the angst and happiness that I felt at that time.

Writing just seemed to take me away from the present day. I got lost in my writing and found especially when I was sitting on a rock near the ravine or really anywhere in nature, my mind would just be set free. I have always had a great imagination, and when pen hit paper, it took off. Many times I have been inspired with stories created in my mind and have not written them down, but hope that newer and better stories will begin to take shape and form.

I have always loved reading and I think through that love, that it inspired me to be a writer. I have just recently got back into writing, and I find that I now carry a notebook just about everywhere I go because it is at the craziest time that a thought enters that I know will take shape or form down the road somewhere.

## Prison Life

Prison life is lonely
In the dark cage
You're trapped
You can't get free
Your emotions send you places
you don't want to be

Darkness sends you everywhere
No light will be seen
You want to escape
to see the world outside.

# *Meena*

# A Glimmer It Was........

A glimmer it was--
was it you
or the sun ?

A chilly winter
blossomed in spring.
Whiffs of the flowers fled,
diffused in the sky.
The rainbow emerged,
half born,
half engulfed,
wonder-struck visions stopped
at the semi-circle.
Near was the horizon
distant was - I.
Closed eyes captured
unfolding emotions
but
the feelings
flowing and flying
endeavouring to touch
the rainbow,
plunging in space
searching
the elusive pot.

Is it the treasure?
Will I find
my lost destiny there
with you beside me?

A destiny-
lost in our hearts
at a time
when the time was
Stillborn.

## A Stillness Moves

Distances fade,
a feeling
as if I touched
the limitless remains.
Quivering fingers
grasp the floating clouds.
They merge in me
as I in you.

The hues of blue
disappear
in each other,
when the sky
re-emerges,
beneath to above
getting wet
by the fresh rain.

My feet soaked
embedded in sand
leave impressions
strong enough
wiping off
the tidal waves
that strike
the climax within.
Sand slips away
under my feet.

A stillness moves
inside me.

Duality will remain
I know,
separating me from you,
yet a dream is instilled,
I pulsate
yearn--

to be fecundated
by the distant you.

## Unrecognizable

Graying evening.
Shades of black fading.
Starkness of night!
Neutrality spread
All over our faces.
Unrecognizable.

What was it?

You recognized
I did not?
Was my vision hazy?
Or I looked at the haze?
Perhaps
We are beginning
a new end.

# ICONOCLAST

Is she a vase
or a statue on a pedestal?

She is no icon!

Her feet strong
firm on ground.
The earth supports her.
The real in her
longs to be
revealed through layers
seeking identifications
undraped
in a figure-less
formless existence.

In vain,
she searches - an iconoclast,
beyond the turbidity of love.

Will she find one in you?

**Instant In Motion**

Trimmings

old and torn

change in

the flowing stress,

a garb,

hard cover,

hiding an instant

to be touched

to be in motion.

## Potency

Thoughts immersed verses.
A rhythmic fantasy
Pondering in the mortal failure;
bursting shadows,
a lifeless poise
potent enough to unite
the clinging poverty of a sterile substance.

## Reverberations

The thrills masquerade
even as they experience
a world of expansion

Far away,
I shrink in a black hole,
Where life searches
For the charismatic remote leisure
seeking a strength
as I stand
face to face
with the deserted truth
A plunging darkness
as bare as death
where a dot
disperses a line
in a voluminous circle,
folding the fire
a living time.
Images annihilate.
The bodiless prevails.

What was it?
That whispered
Reverberations
in a chilled silence.

## Strangers

In the day's heat
I sought myself in you.
Strangers we were still are
silhouettes in each other's eyes.
Remnants of a deflected time.
Monotony
Nonexistence is
claustrophobic.

I fear remaining an outline.
Your warmth lingers
uncaptured,
fading into opacity.
I know 1 will burn
till the fire burns in me.

## Tangled In Time

Past, Present, Future
Dusty Barricades,
Symbols dissolve
I plunge back,
float and delve.
But,
I stick to the moist damp earth
fearing devastation.

My mouth is full of clay.
Is it the smell of the soil that I eat?
The dry coarse earth?
Is that me?
The streams swim in my eyes.
Visions divide.
The sight freezes in the silent snow.
North wind hovers
tangled in time.

## The evolution of literature and languages
## of ethnic descent and the changing environment.

Language and culture are inter-woven in our normal lives but that depth or the centre point, from where all the imagination and creativity originate in the form of art and literature are obscured in the hidden layers of the unconscious self. It is the deepest layer of the self from where all the diversity of life springs from and at the same time it is the focal point or an ultimate abode of all the diverseness into oneness of the being.

The essence of a language lies in its literary merits which in turn influences and impacts its literature and literary capabilities. One wonders that what these literary merits are and from where and how do they surface? Any literary work, poetry or prose, which represents the high quality of artistic merit, will create a standard and an everlasting place for itself in enhancing the quality of that particular language.

Keeping all this in mind, is it not the responsibility of all the literary organizations, specifically ethnic to embrace the global and technological change so that they are well positioned and equipped to support and become helpful in the initiation and the continuity of the artistic quality and its expression in a language and in a way, that it becomes individualized and its influence directly or indirectly can impact and be showcased in the contemporary literary stream? This is the literature which is coming into being through the contribution of immigrant population of varied ethnic languages in Canada and many other countries.

Any good literature has new-ness in it. This new-ness comes with changing thought in a changing environment. This probably indicates that the thought process and day to day interactions are directly linked with the usage of our language but the quality of language depends on the literary capabilities and it's artistic merit.

Immigrant population has always been extremely sensitive to the change which gives an opportunity to bring new-ness in the literary arts. So it becomes very important that the literary merit which is dependent on its artistic abilities is also kept alive while embracing the change. This is evident for the survival of the ethnic literature along with the language in which it is written.

It is natural for the literary artist to feel and cherish the intimacy with the life stream and nature within the depth of the soul. And in time the very feel and touch of these creative moments which got obscured and entrapped in the maze of life and its mundanity, surface to the conscious levels of mind in the form of language arts or for that matter in any other art form.
A question rises as to what kind of relationship does self-expression have with the language in this fast developing world of technological change and globalization? Also how is it affecting the human sensibilities and the creative process? What could be the primary medium of expression of artistic literary abilities? Is that the form of language itself is going through an extreme radical change?

## Changing Environment & Its Influences
In this fast pace of changing environment, will Hindi, Urdu and many other ethnic languages be able to remain in their original forms and if yes, then till when? Is it not that Hindi, Urdu, Punjabi and many other ethnic languages need to have a new direction? If the language has to remain alive and go ahead, then is it not necessary that we embrace this inevitable change individually and bring back the vibrancy in the language? Is it not the utter need of these changing times? This change is compelling us to find a focal point in all the kind of diversity which rises from caste, creed, cultures, traditions, and also with contemporary technological changes, a common playground where there is an exchange and sharing of thoughts. In today's environment, it is necessary to join hands with the diversity surrounding us to grow and co-exist. And this is challenging too. If observed carefully, this is the predicament of any ethnic language in the fast paced environment today. Let alone the ethnic languages even the English language is also not spared from this change. The effects of this change are shown largely

on the traditional form of English where the idiom and the usage are being changed radically and continuously.

The changing environment and the youth want that which can give an instant stimulation to their finer sensibilities, something which they can understand in a glance. Meaning powerful, pictorial images and visuals accompanied by sound effects and maybe few words of a prevalent language which can give some sensible and in-depth meaning to their enquiring minds. The times are of multitasking and speed. Therefore Hindi, Urdu or any other language that wants to get ahead will have to catch the speed of 'SMS's and will have to be breaking free from the archaic bandages. It will have to embrace new experiments and diversity. Not only this, an understanding of the reactions of the subconscious nature of this diversity with the conscious nature mind. This may help in giving a new direction in the expression of the subtle sensibilities in a newer medium and environment to the literary arts and then the language can get a new meaning. I think it is a very big challenge of the changing times for us but at the same time an opportunity for the literary arts.

# *Marijana*

## Marijana's Story

At this very second, go back to your favourite moment. Remember the smells, the colours, the sounds around you. Remember who was with you or if you were alone. Remember how you felt – probably full of joy, exhilaration, anticipation, maybe even a little fear? Taste that memory and let it roll around in your head, in your heart, let it enter your limbs and fill you with warmth, with peace.

That favourite moment is what writing is for me. Some call it "the natural high". I am not sure how or where or why it started. It kind of just happened.

Snowflakes for me were never just snowflakes. They were jewels that lit up the night sky in my back yard, the lace of the gods, the immaculate harbingers of winter.

And people were never just people. They were and are stories that compel me to put pen to paper, type on my laptop or furiously scribble lines on a napkin in some small café in my neighbourhood.

Although I don't know why I am compelled to write, I never want to stop. And I never will.

## To "The One"

falling off the pedestals
tumble off the high thrones in each other's eyes
the shine now gone, dullness underneath
causality of time
our feelings roll around
tumbleweeds
the world comes down
crashes with gentle brutality
around our feet

my mauled heart is no longer blind
you, an illusion of the sun
spirited sparkle that never reaches its
intended path
only a sliver of light
 a sliver of light

## The Blank Page

The clichés well up inside me
pound their tiny fists against my brain
moan, whine, cajole to get out
and tell the world
how strong, smart, stupid we are
in allowing their existence
let them roll off our tongues
like drops of water

I close my eyes

semblance of no sight
will bring insight
intense
bubbles in a Perrier bottle
at that French restaurant
where you kissed me
and I forgot to hate my life

as I ponder this
a word comes
simple, elegant
slides, builds rhythms inside my head
waltzes into my memory

and then another

and another

soon it's a watershed
maelstrom of thoughts,
wishes, dreams

regrets
I am not the captain anymore;
instead a vessel, adorned with eyes
ears, hands
to deliver an epitaph

the ink has stained my fingers
I gasp
a message rolls inward
with my breath

# The Road (excerpt) Chapter One

Flipping through the latest edition of the local newspaper, I look for an ad Jenny told me she placed. It's there, on the last page. Short and succinct: a name, physical description, what he wore last, where he was last seen.

I sip the cold mint tea, swirling a bit of it around in my mouth, tasting the nuances and subtleties.

I then check my email.

I am trying to remain calm about this but it's hard.

Two days. It's been two days since the ad appeared and the email Jenny provided as point of contact had produced only spam. The particularly interesting one was about tips on how to seduce anyone from your crush to your grandmother.

Frowning at the screen, I once again pick up my I Love New York mug – the tea now leaves an acrid taste in my mouth.

This is getting me nowhere.

The cramping in my legs reminds me that I should stop turning down dates with my Stairmaster. I get up and walk over to the window of my flat on Lakeshore Road to get the blood pumping again.

Aptly named, Lakeshore Road faces the lake, which, at the moment, churns, and rolls like a heavy wild beast, the strong wind tugging at the waves and then smashing them against the hapless looking rocks. As Jenny said, when we spoke last night, nature was being a real bitch this year. I prefer to think of her as an old hag, teasing us with hints of spring but all under the guise of never-ending winter.

My shoulders relax at the thought of a similar paradox of my friend's sweet natured appearance and the loud mouth that could make any sailor blush. I catch the reflection of the newspaper lying primly next to my laptop and I tense again.

Jenny tells me that any missing person's case has its challenges. The clientele that walk through my best friend's office door already have best friends of their own, namely jealousy, vanity and greed. Not to mention that 90 percent of the time, people that she looks for do not want to be found.

But the worst clients are the sad ones. Anxious parents, coming to her, begging her, in tears, to find their children, when they have exhausted all other avenues, including trying to meet with drug dealers that they somehow found out used to supply their kids.

But the case Jenny took on this past week was different. Certainly, different for me. It involved someone from my past, someone of whom I had buried all thoughts, so deep inside myself, that sometimes I wondered if he ever existed at all.

My brain refused to say his name out loud but I knew it, like I knew my own heart. Half smiling to myself, I remember the line from Oscar Wilde's poem: *"Yet each man kills the thing he loves"*

The knock at my front door is hard and raspy, as if coming from aging knuckles. I walk through my foyer, feeling the morning chill of the wooden floor panels on my bare feet. I peep through the peephole. All I see is darkness, meaning that the person on the other side of that door is also peeping through the peephole.

"Delivery!" Thick, possibly Eastern European accent, very gruff, seems to come from someone who's probably been a smoker for decades.

"You Regina King?"

I haven't heard anyone call me that in years.

"I wasn't expecting a package", sweeping a few errant strands of my hair out of my face, I check my t-shirt for any possible mishaps and then reach for the door handle.

"Lady, that none of my business. I leave it in front but you need to sign."

Then, a short but deep, guttural cough. Definitely a smoker.

Opening the door slowly, yet firmly, I face a rotund yet surprisingly tall man with heavyset eyes. The top of his bald head gives off an eerie glow against the hallway lights. Instinctively, I take a small step back into my doorway.

He thrusts a package at me, which looks more like a moving box than a neat, tidily labeled FedEx packages I get when ordering from eBay. Before I know it, the clipboard is in my hand.

"Sign", he thrusts a pen at me with the same force he handed me the package,

"Okay, okay". Before I could question why he doesn't have a one of those electronic signing pads, he walks away, faster than expected, as though he is late for an appointment of some kind.

The box feels heavy which serves as another reminder that I should visit the gym more often. Although being a financial analyst doesn't require a lot of stamina, I have always believed that exercise helps clear the mind. And clear mind is a requirement when helping Jenny with her case research.

Jenny certainly needs both the clear mind and the stamina in her line of work. You need to be fast when you are running after someone, usually your missing persons.

I managed to place the box on my kitchen table, jamming it between my half eaten breakfast and the horrendous blue vase I keep only because my father gave it to me after one of his travels, promising that it is supposed to bring me wealth and fertility. I am still waiting for both. Okay, more for the wealth.

I find myself doing a 360 around the table, focusing on the package I just received. It's brown, plain, moving type of box, taped with standard thick gray tape. No return address.

Should I open it now?

Not finding a letter opener, I move over to my kitchen drawers and finally find a pair of scissors. Pausing, biting my lip, I stare at the box and think of what kind of questions Jenny would ask. For example, who, these days, sends this type of package? A grandmother, a wife of an incarcerated prisoner? What is in the box? Is it a finger, an ear, maybe someone's head?

My phone burrs, breaking me out of my increasingly morbid thoughts.

"Hey babe!"

"Hey", Hunter's gruff voice always reminds me why I love dating musicians. Of course, it doesn't hurt that Hunter believes that one should take care of one's body as well as one's voice.

Suddenly, my gram's voice is like a blitz in my head. I can almost see her out in the Arizona desert waving her finger at my five year old self telling me that a virile man needs a strong headed woman and you, Regina, will grow up to be a strong headed woman.

I believe gram's may not necessarily approve of my choice.

As I listen to Hunter talk about his gig last night, my gray blue eyes stare back at me from the mirror and I find my gaze slowly travelling down my body.

I am in good shape, but I work hard for that. My style could do with a make over but my staple has always been and will always be blue jeans and funky t-shirts. Today, my shirt says, Impossible is Nothing.

I have to remember that no one can see the scars. It's been years and even without clothes, the scars are barely visible.

I hear Hunter repeat something, sounding annoyed that I am not listening.

"The Long Hall? Fifteen minutes? "

# *Mark*

### Mark's Story

When one is learning a language, a first or second one, I was told to use a particular word in three different sentences.

Most of the time one can retain that new word for life. Writing one sentence down, then asking oneself if one can use a better word to convey the idea in a more descriptive manner, one can feel great seeing this innovation where none existed before. A sense of accomplishment is achieved at no cost to anyone.

I write to enjoy this daily euphoria.

# When Nature Calls

"Melissa! Where are you?" James held onto the bicycle as he peered into every corner of the school yard. Why meet here? She could have told him on the telephone. What if someone saw them together?

From the leafy, green bushes, she beckoned him to join her.

"What's so urgent? I got here as fast as I could." The bike was becoming such a massive weight; he dropped it, barely missing his feet.

Her head was down, no smile across her sweet lips, indicating something serious. She looked every each way but directly at him. This only made him more anxious.

"We cannot see each other anymore" she finally blurted out. "I am getting married next month." It was easier to say than she had imagined it would be. After all, she had played the scene in her mind for many days.

James reached out to her, not quite quick enough, as she backed away furiously.

"What have I done wrong? I thought we had a good thing going. It was good but now it is over. I have to start a new life with someone else."

"So I was just a stand-in`, a piece of meat until you could find a different entrée? Why did you even have sex with me all these years?"

Down went her eyes so he would not see her trying to hold back the tears. One time, she considered telling him that he could have been a father, twice. Now, it would make the situation worse.

"Well, you know, I had these urges, calls of nature." She wanted to turn the table on him. "Did you not have the same natural urges as me? You never refused my advances as I recall."

"That's why I thought we made a wonderful couple. We both loved being together, doing everyday stuff and capping the day off with sex. Was it not good for you?"

"Always! But it is not enough. You remember when we went to the parade and I had a different call of nature? You found me…" she hesitated.

"A Johnny of the Spot? Yes, it is still quite vivid in my mind. So, you used me to satisfy your inclinations, regardless of their importance, and now, you want to flush me down the toilet?"

She did not want to prolong this agony, sidestepping the bike; she turned around and picked up her foot. The whisper was soft, but emphatic.

"No more, at least, not for the foreseeable future."

# How to Take a Shower

Warning:  do not take off our clothes!  This is not for perverts, about perverts or by a pervert.
If you are already naked, put something on, like the radio.  You can take your hand off the knob.

Now, though most showers are strictly solo, occasionally, there has been another person in the same stall, at the same instance as me.  This is justified by her desire to save water, money and arousal time.  She has calculated that she has shaved at least one half hour from what she euphemistically calls pillow talk, and this is from someone who failed math in kindergarten.

Bliss and harmony, this arrangement has enabled her to wrap up the entire procedure in the least amount of time without any loss of enjoyment.  After one such session, sleep overcame me before I could count up the five kangaroos.  Why kangaroos instead of sheep?  Logic! They can jump higher, faster and further than sheep, mainly because they are not fattened up before slaughter.

Normally, I think about what I am going to write the next day.  I had to give up the wishful and unrewarding practice of imagining myself with no less than five young, beautiful, and sexy women due to her uncanny ability to read my mind.  Unbridled lust, horrendous betrayal and miserable infidelity were just a few of the choice words she heaved and heaped upon me.  Informing her that she was also included in any wild and uninhibited romp of pleasure only caused her to redouble her assault upon my now black, blue and red body.

I could sense and feel that no amount of feminine wiles would be able to penetrate my dreams of carnal delight.  This person appeared, alone, bathed in some sort of aura with a light display greater than any aurora borealis.  In a somber but gentle manner, he spoke as I always envisioned how my creator would address anyone.

"Young man!" He said. Of course, to him even an old man like me could pass for an age of no greater than a millionth of a microsecond.

"You don't know this," he continued, "but you are no longer in my book of life. Rather, you are slated to leave everyone and everything soon. I am going to give you a parting gift. Most of the people I select in the book of death come to me after passing away at home. For you, I have decided to let you enjoy your last moments in a shower. Any requests?"

"Thank you for that consideration," I replied "Any chance of some guests joining me on my final farewell?"

"No problem! Choose!"

"How about Shakira, Katy Perry and Beyonce?"

"Only three? I thought you were all fired up and could handle five women?"

"I am leaving the other two for my wife!"

# Sense and Nonsense

Jane, eyes bulging, blonde hair wilting, face red, not from the gentle sun, but from the eruption of blood pressure within every vessel of her body, entered the small neat kitchen of her childhood home. By doing so, she let in the pervasive, smokey aroma from the barbecue.

"How dare you?" she challenged immediately after she closed the door. "What right do you have for saying we are trying for a child?" Pouting engorged lips capable of a sensuality rivaled only by a few other women, none in attendance outdoors here for the celebration of the first year of marriage between her and Daniel.

Though he was thirty centimetres taller than her and twice her weight, her forcefulness, her directness, her single-mindedness of purpose, gave her a strength disproportionate to her petiteness.

What was he to do? He stayed as far away as possible within the confines of the room. He could not deny that he had said what she had just repeated for all the family and friends to hear through the thin walls of the old house. Not admitting to what she considered a mistake, would only anger her more. He gripped the edge of the counter, slightly sticky from all the cooking he had done by himself.

"Why would I ever want a child with you? I was on the pill for months before we got married. Did you think you were my first? What a fool you are, a very stupid fool! Here, choke on this!" her voice escalated to a feverish pitch. "I have been pregnant twice, and you were not the father!" She rested her back upon the wall, exhausted. From the strain of this revelation, rivulets of sweat ran down those puffy cheeks.

If Mount Everest had fallen directly upon him, it would have been a blessing. He reeled at this assault on all he held to be sacred and inviolable. No amount of atonement could reverse the consequences of her indiscretions. Straightening up from his cowardly stance, he limped across the minefield that was the kitchen floor, and went outside to encounter further embarrassments.

The Beach Boys were right – he was a prisoner of his own device. How was he supposed to shake off this atrocity against his manhood? Would he ever forgive her? Could he let everything slide? He had touched her, but in retrospect, only superficially.

Kindness depleted, delayed, kindness deemed detrimental, kindness destroyed. Is there a place where kindness is stored, to be called upon and withdrawn as needed?

Daniel had no immediate answer. For the first time in his life, he regretted that he not only knew his spouse from the time they were children, but from now on, he actually hated her.

# *Milena*

# Milena's Story

I was born in Romania to parents Ileana and Eugen. I grew up in a rich cultural tradition, in a family that values literature, philosophy and the arts. In my childhood I was an avid reader and I enjoyed authors as diverse as Epictetus, Marcus Aurelius, Kant, Schopenhauer, Richard Feynman and Werner Heisenberg. I have had a keen interest in mathematics, sciences and computers, as well as humanities.

I had many influential teachers, some of whom recommended outstanding books which changed my way of thinking. However, the most influential figure was my father, an erudite with encyclopedic interests. He transferred some of his passions to me: music is definitely an important component in a rich texture of intertwining interests.

I started writing after leaving my country of origin, inspired by the discovery of the adoptive world as well as the longing for the places and people left behind. In my first book I described the archaic ways of living which are still present in the Romanian countryside, where traditional values are perpetuated through generations; I juxtaposed them to the dynamism of the new world.

I am captivated by the new perspectives offered by my travels, as well as other recent discoveries. I am particularly interested in understanding our own thinking processes; it taught me a great deal about myself and others. I would be very interested to explore this topic in my next books.

To me, writing is a way to explore new ideas. Because I don't feel constrained by self-imposed rules, I explore freely. For me, a blank page is not intimidating; it is my sandbox where I enjoy playing, experimenting and innovating new ways of communication.

When asked what I wanted to accomplish in life, I once said: "I have accomplished most of my dreams. I plan to continue making a difference and give back. I'd like to write a few notable books that show the intensity of my colours and project a fresh perspective on life. Last but not least, I'd love to contribute to a world of mutual understanding, respect and love".

In my spare time, I teach at the University of Toronto or spend time with my family. Alex, my son, is a student at Yale University and Marin, my husband, is a Professor at York University, here in Toronto.

# To India and back

Although I acquired the visa to go to India with my husband, I never accomplished this dream.

Someone told me that I stayed home and waited for him to come back, just like Penelope, wife of Ulysses, did. I had anticipated his departure and got through it feverishly. I prepared him for the long, hard journey by cooking spicy food before his trip, for him to get used to. The night before he left, I dressed in a long, colorful floral skirt. I sang and danced in Bollywood style, as I wanted him to know I'd be waiting for him to return.

He ventured to India in the midst of a big heat wave. His first message only announced he'd arrived safely and checked in to his hotel room. He planned to remain inside and prepare for his presentation. The next day I heard the same thing. The third day he mentioned that he stepped outside for only ten minutes, but the heat hit him like a shovel. "I hope that tomorrow I will be able to stay outside for fifteen minutes" he said. I was happy to hear that his presentation went well, that it had sparked the interest of the international scientific community. He later reported the discovery of the town, where Google, Microsoft and some of India's best universities are located.

I wondered if I would have liked the trip to India and enjoyed the adventure of discovering this new world. Oh, yes, I would have loved it. However, I would not have enjoyed being stuck close to the technological companies or as a prisoner in the hotel. The business hub of the city was too far from India's soul.
I was told that the five-star hotel checks the luggage the same way as the airport. Taxis are inspected underneath because they fear explosives. That part, for sure, I wouldn't have liked. Besides, I would have felt guilty at a luxurious hotel when those who maintained the property were walking barefoot and carried loads on their heads. However, I would have loved to be able to sightsee and discover the city on my own terms. I heard that foreign tourists do not usually go out by themselves; much less a woman alone. Each must be escorted by taxis and guides and

needs to be advised by local people to understand how things work in these new surroundings.

For a while I was happy that I stayed home, to avoid the heat wave that hit India at that time. I watched, detached, literally and figuratively, the news coverage, delivered by his emails. Later, I waited anxiously to hear of his safe arrival to New Delhi after another flight.

I accompanied him, virtually, through his visit to Taj Mahal, an unimaginable splendor. "Once you see the Taj Mahal, there's nothing else that you can admire. After seeing it, you better go home," he told me. However, later in his visit he discovered another beauty, the fort of Agra.

I learned that despite the heat and many flights, he continued to work hard on a project, until he left New Delhi. The day of his departure, he needed to check out early from his hotel room and he had no air conditioned place to go to. The temperature in the shade reached forty seven degrees Celsius. I worried how he'd handle the heat. His flight wasn't supposed to depart until two o'clock in the morning, next day. I confided to a friend that I was worried about him; she comforted me. She assured me that I have nothing to fear. He'll manage. But I did not find comfort in his message: "I really hope it's true that what doesn't kill you makes you stronger." I was then thankful I hadn't gone with him, as I couldn't have tolerated the heat.

However, I doubted my decision when I looked at the beautiful pictures that revealed a colorful and fascinating country. Regretfully, I observed that my husband could enjoy a great trip without me at his side. I had believed that only I could plan a trip well and take great pictures. This time it turned out to prove I'm not indispensable, although my husband insisted the trip would have been better if I had travelled with him. I wonder if his statement was just a kindness of sorts and nothing more. I noticed that the more I discovered India through his eyes, the more I grew unsure if I'd made the right decision. Regrets grew with every picture I was receiving. I finally realized that I failed to take a rare opportunity to travel in that part of the world.

Although I was not with him, I felt I accompanied him throughout the trip; even when he stopped in Frankfurt on his way back. He was surprised when I answered his email immediately. It was three o'clock in the morning in Toronto.

I could not meet him at the airport but when we did I felt the warmth from his loving hug. His greeting was: "I missed you. I missed the gym and the berries." I did not know whether to rejoice or not. I seemed to be mixed into an odd company of things he'd missed during his absence. I did know I was at the top of his list, irrespective of what else he lacked while he was away. He seemed happy to be back home to recount his adventures.

I felt that he was deeply moved by what he had discovered. Humbled with his observation of how little we knew about India. Although I read the tales of the Mahabharata in my childhood, I don't know the bare essential about this country. I don't know who fought the wars, erected the most amazing architectural wonders, or the waves of history that swept the country. My husband was surprised by the complexity of this foreign world, and its blatant juxtaposition of extreme poverty and opulent richness. "Poverty is more severe than any poverty worldwide. We're talking about millions and millions of souls – hundreds of millions? - living in slums." He was moved by the kindness of the people and surprised to discover their soft side. Then the arts: music and dance, as well as other exciting discoveries I learned second-hand.

My husband was astonished by the Indian technological marvels. There are old discoveries that showcase their native sense of innovation. Their creativity revealed places and forms from techniques used for intarsia gemstones, marble lattices at Taj Mahal and novel ways to channel the water, as well as smart approaches to filter the light in this famous architectural jewel.

He then talked about the acoustic quality carried out around the

Hyderabad Fort, where one could communicate to the top of the hill when one spoke softly. Outstanding acoustics allowed those to get closer to the fort and communicate through short claps carried by the wind at the top of the hill. Those inside the fort heard them and allowed visitors to enter. The conversation took place, through an ingenious clapping alphabet, long before the Morse code was invented.

As a specialist in complex adaptive systems, my husband is invited as a keynote speaker at international conferences. He continues to be amazed at the natural adaptability of many systems and mechanisms in India. For example, the movement of the Indian intersections. The traffic is an excellent example of adaptive system that functions almost optimally – although it is self-regulated. Apparently, there are not many rules on the road, even for the busiest intersections, where everyone comes from all sides. It seems that these intersections are surprisingly effective... not only did they not trample each other, but there are very few traffic jams.

Drivers seem to adapt well to last minute road conditions. I know I could not drive there. But this is a clear example that illustrates the wisdom of groups not governed in a conscious way. They seem guided by a divine hand or a collective eye. Indians give us lessons about circumstantial and adaptive collective intelligence. It seems to replace the need of a higher coordination. Is it the same principle used to communicate between smaller entities such as neurons in a more complex organism, similar maybe to the human brain? Or the bees from hives? Ants from anthills?

The above comparisons do not include the North American intersections that are too predictable to count in this discussion. In North America the script is simplified, because the traffic rules represent the law. In India the system is not as regulated: it is more chaotic and yet it seems to be quite effective despite the fact that it is based on circumstantial solutions that seem to somehow work, in a rather predictable way. I marvel how this comes together in an almost deterministic fashion. Enough talk about adaptive systems and their real-time reaction to the ever-changing circumstances.

My husband continued to tell the story of the last days in New Delhi when it was forty-seven degrees in the shade. He explained how scorched pavement and buildings walls radiated heat like a furnace. When the warm wind blew, the hotter it became. During the temple visit, Indians were circulating on small marble paths instead of going on the pavement. Why? Indian walk barefoot in the scorching summer days but they cannot walk on hot stone which burns like fire. They built narrow marble paths inside their temples. This allows them to go barefoot in the sun as they wait their turn to enter the shadowed building for prayer. I wondered if they pray for colder days. I guess so. I imagine that when one walks on the marble tiles, one moves from one foot to the other, to quench the heated feet.

As my husband told his stories, I visualized counts of cows, horses, camels, goats, sheep and monkeys. They seem to be coexisting peacefully with motorcycles, tricycles and cars in the Indian cities. They all paraded before me. I pictured myself in cramped spaces with beggars: I felt surrounded, as in the Hitchcock movie *The Birds*, threatened on all sides by flocks of birds.

He then revealed the scene of some people defecating along the riverside while others washed two feet away... I learned that many are praying to die near the Ganges so that their ashes get scattered over the waves of the river ... where decomposed or swollen corpses are floating ... It amazes me how, despite the violation of the hygienic rules, as we know them, Indians cleanse themselves in ways completely foreign to us. I wonder, perhaps, if the waters of the Ganges have some miraculous properties or if the spices they eat help cut the evil from the roots. I guess this is one of India's secrets. I wonder how so many survive despite all hazards. I am sure that we have many lessons to learn from them in regards to natural medicine and their understanding about the human body. Both physically and mentally. I've also learned that India gave birth to religions that have proven viable to take root across the world. For example, their various forms of meditation have embraced followers around the world.

I'm sorry to have not recorded my husband's account about his last day in Delhi as the museums were closed. He was forced to walk the streets under the unbearable heat until he discovered a magic place mentioned by the tourist guides, Hazrat Nizamuddin Dargah. This is where the devoted Muslims sing qawwalis in memory of Hazrat Nizamuddin Auliya (1238-1325), who is considered a saint.

My husband had a Hindu guide, a man with a sharp sense of humor who wondered why he should go there. As it was mandatory to take one's shoes off, he wondered if there was a risk to leave the place barefoot. The guide initially informed my husband that he will not accompany him during his visit, but he eventually decided to keep him company: he opened his way among the many Muslims pooled in that area. One asked why they were there. On this account I felt fear since I knew that their path crossed some kind of a bazaar. My husband was terrified that someone would take his camera, but nothing like that happened. When they reached their destination, they discovered a divine music that made it worth the visit.

The Hindu asked him if he liked the music. The guide confessed to not having set foot on the place in more than twenty years. The tomb could be seen under several conditions: one being barefoot and another being a man; one with a turban. My husband had to remain with the women at the entrance of the tomb. Barefoot, I was, he reported, but I didn't have a turban. I guess he could have addressed his shortcoming if he could have found a turban. For me, however, the situation would have been hopeless. I wouldn't have been allowed to enter no matter what I did. My segregation would have been final and irrevocable. I was just a woman. We looked at the pictures of my husband bareheaded among the women covered in bright colors. The fact that their heads were covered was not enough for them to be granted the right of passage to visit the tomb.

Then, all of a sudden, my husband pointed out his companion. A big man one could count on for protection. The man ensured his security during his stay in New Delhi.

My husband mentioned that if I'd visited the country I would need an entire year to write about it. He was right. He made reference to the colors, music, odors and the overall contrasts of the place. The food. The temples. I was left with regret that I missed important lessons and an experience that would have moved me deeply.

At least I had mentally exercised the discovery of this amazing place beyond direct contact, in ways that reveal its wonder.

His story ended as it began, with dismay of how little we know about India and how fascinating their world is. He was shaken to the core. He obviously had been impressed by the spectacular world he'd discovered.

I secretly hope that he is happy to be back home, to his lady who would dance again in Bollywood style.

## Life as it is

It is said that every morning the sun rises over Africa; every gazelle knows it must run faster than the fastest lion. As every lion knows it must run faster than the slowest gazelle. In short – everyone tries to make the most of each day to catch the next sunrise.

For too long, I awoke every morning anxious about the day I needed to win. I ran enough to survive and enjoy a few gorgeous sunrises. I ran quite fast. For the longest time, I ran like a gazelle. For quite some time now I stopped running long stretches. Sometimes, I wonder if I can sprint at all.

Lately, I seem to find my comfort in writing, in front of a blank page. The only running I still do is to compose small prose in my head, some of which remains unwritten, unspoken confessions. I sometimes sink into reverie and I wonder what effect it has on my competitive edge. I wonder how many sunrises will I still survive in this jungle ruled by the wild competition, where I feel and more, just a prey?

## Mount Pleasant Cemetery

I always liked the *Mount Pleasant Cemetery* in Toronto with his old trees in a park-like setting. In the past, I took leisurely strolls in search of refuge, comfort and peace. I used to sit for hours next to a small tree, watching it flourish. I used to feel part of a divine spectacle.

This year, however the show was not the same. It seemed amplified by a new meaning. It was Easter and I was standing next to my father's grave. It was a warm and sunny day, and I was surrounded by the Spring scents and chirping birds.

Scottish bagpipe music played in the background added a special melancholy to the scene. The piper walked around my father's grave in an equal, measured and musical pace. A faint sound of beauty and peace were left behind, as well as our sorrow.

# *Scott*

# A Long, Strange Trip

I've always been creative but I didn't take up writing until 2006. Before that, I had drawn with pencil and painted with acrylics until about 1995. That year, I met my wonderful wife and, as you might guess, I wanted to spend my free time with her. Life, being what it is, took the course it took for another decade before the creative urge returned. My wife and I went to an art supply store and bought about $200 of paints, canvas and an easel. However, my heart wasn't in it. I didn't know why and struggled with it until 2006 when a co-worker (and good friend) tried her hand at writing a historical romance.

Something clicked. I wanted to write. Never mind I hadn't written anything for fun EVER and nothing of any kind since my university days (the early 80's). It felt right, so I started. My first work was a 220,000 word behemoth. I found writing groups and joined them. Most critical was the Heart of Carolina Romance Writers. They are a wonderful group, very welcoming, with newcomers sitting next to 20-time NY Times bestsellers. All I knew was I knew almost nothing about writing. In hindsight, I think that was a blessing because I didn't have any of the usual bad habits that most novices do.

The other big aid was finding two fantastic critique partners, Connie and Shirley. Very helpful and supportive, they became close friends, despite none of us ever having met. Connie lives in Australia and writes fantasy. Shirley writes crime mysteries in Alabama. Through hard work and their invaluable input, my writing improved dramatically.

There is one other detail that helped my writing and, although I mention it, I don't recommend trying it. When the recession hit the US in 2008, I lost my job and stayed unemployed for two years. The stress and anguish came out in my writing, a therapy of sorts that helped me keep my sanity through the darkest time of my life.

Now in 2015, I will have my debut novel, *Quite The Catch*, published. I look back at my writing life and a line from a favorite song comes to mind: *"What a long, strange trip it's been ..."*

# Contributors

*Elizabeth Banfalvi* teaches workshops on meditation and stress. She is an author of a meditation book series and short stories and is published on Yahoo, Apple, Amazon and Balboa Press. Website: *www.elizabethbanfalvi.com*

*Scott Berger* writes for the love of it and takes great pleasure from ignoring most writing advice. Through a passion for storytelling, the good fortune to meet and know so many wonderfully talented writers, and the unwavering belief God looks after fools, Scott's debut novel, a romantic suspense titled *Quite The Catch,* is expected in the fall of 2015. He affords his passion by being an architect in the daytime, living outside Toronto with his very understanding wife Rita and their Rottweiler child, Puppy.
Website: *https://www.facebook.com/bergernewromsuspense*

*Meena Chopra* is a visual artist, author and educator with a background in media and advertising. She has widely exhibited her art all over the world and authored and writes and published 2 poetry books in Hindi, English & Urdu. She writes in Hindi and English and was translated in German. She has co-edited a multilingual poetry e-book of Canadian poets written in Hindi & Urdu called "RANG AUR NOOR" (COLOURS & RADIANCE). Her writings and poetry have been published in many well-known literary journals which includes, "American Diversity Report "and she is a regular blogger in Hindi and English. She has been recipient of many recognitions and awards in poetry, community and arts.
Website: *http://meenachopra17.wix.com/meena-chopra-artist*

*Angela Ford's* love for words keeps the page turning. She's internationally known for bestselling suspense and contemporary romance. Angela is a proud member of the RWA and Mississauga Writers Group.
Website: *www.angelafordauthor.com*

*Mark David Garden* has completed one book and is working on his second. During retirement he feels it is imperative to keep his mind and body active. Looking up new words or the correct spelling often leads to new ideas or innovative ways to state a sentence. By doing some research, one can expand the field that may have been narrow but is now wider and more comprehensive.

*Marijana Gmitrovic* is an aspiring writer who migrated to Canada from her native Serbia in 1988. For many years, her main focus has been writing poetry. She is currently working on her first thriller/mystery novel.

*John Henderson* is a Registered Marriage (RMFT, OAMFT) & Sex Therapist with an Oakville, ON practice specializing in Couple Relationship Repair (marriage counselling) , anxiety , depression, sex and internet addictions, male & female arousal and sexual dysfunctions. John's motivational speaking and writing focus on positive growth and personal resiliency. Website: *www.hendersoncounselling.com 905 847-0955*

*Kim MacMurray* work full time as a Development Officer for an Albertan municipality. My passion and other job is as a spiritual reader and reiki practitioner. I also manage Kimmi's Reading and Reiki on Facebook where I offer a daily reading. I am a married mother of two wonderful boys. My passions are yoga, reading, essential oils and all things metaphysical. Website: *www.facebook.com/KimmisReadingsandReiki*

*Hamzah Moin* is a satirical writer and entertainer. He created Maniac Muslim, an award-winning Muslim humour blog and is now focusing on writing his first novel, tentatively titled Randomly Selected. Website: *http://www.hamzahmoin.com http://fb.com/maniacmuslim*

*Joseph A. Monachino* is married and his hobbies include writing, reading, and exercising. He graduated from Sheridan College certified in Sales & Marketing and presently works as a manufacturing plant assembler.
Website: *www.transportingdevicestory.weebly.com*

*Milena Munteanu* authored two books: "Far Away" and "From the Land of the Rising Sun". She has a permanent column with the Romanian magazine "Observatorul" and is a frequent collaborator of other cultural publications. Milena is included in multiple anthologies in Romanian, English, Spanish and Italian. She won multiple awards, including the Grand Prize for Literary Reportage, at the "Ciprian Porumbescu" International Festival of the Arts in 2013.
Website: *milena_v26@yahoo.com*

*Daniela Oana* From Romania to Quebec and finally to Ontario, Daniela Oana's poetry romanticizes sorrow, tragedy and death. Daniela shows a particular delight in traditional poetry. Through poetry slams and poetry courses, contemporary poems begin to emerge in her more recent work. Despite her love for creative writing, Daniela studied Journalism-Print and hopes to soon publish her first poetry book.
Website: *http://danielaoana1.wix.com/poet*

*Jasmine Sawant* has been writing essays, articles and short stories while in India. An award-winning alumnus of the post-graduate journalism program of Bhavan's Rajendra Prasad Institute of Communication, Mumbai, Jasmine has been writing and co-writing plays for stage and scripts for commercials. She is the Co-Founder and Artistic Co-Director of SAWITRI Theater Group, Mississauga, that annually produces and presents plays on issues of social and cultural relevance and has written and directed some of these plays, of which, *The Kallus Next Door*, was published in *Word Fest*, the first anthology of the Mississauga Writers' Group, and was part of INSPIRE! Toronto International Book Fair. Her play, *One World Our World*, a dance-theater piece for children, premiered in 2009 and was remounted in June 2015. She is one of the founding members of

the Mississauga Writers' Group.
Website: *http://www.jasminesawant.com/*

*G. Ian Stout* lives with wife Sharon and two white cats in Mississauga while writing story number four, a historical novel spanning more than two thousand years. He'll soon travel to Israel for further research. Ian's third book, *Murder Unedited,* is now available around the world.
Website: *www.writerstout.com*

*Hans Victor von Maltzahn*, the author of the well received, *"THE BLACK SUN ASCENDANT: An Assassins Tale"* (2011), was born in Dublin, Ireland, and raised in North York, Ontario, Canada. An author of poetry and non-fiction, Hans became serious about fiction in 2006 when he started to write the *Black Sun* book series. He has just completed *"AN EARTH ECLIPSED: An Assassin's Revenge"* (2014), Book Two in the series, and has begun the last book in the series, tentatively entitled, *"A BRILLIANT DAWN: An Assassin's Redemption"*. He currently lives in Mississauga, Ontario, Canada with his wife Joanne.
Website: **https://www.amazon.com/author/hansv_vonmaltzahn**
**www.smashwords.com/profile/view/hansvonmaltzahn**

# Copyright Acknowledgements

*Hamzah Moin 2015*

5. **Hans**
Han's Story *Copyright @ Hans Victor von Maltzahn 2015*
The Torn Page, *Copyright @ Hans Victor von Maltzahn 2014*
The Interview *Copyright @ Hans Victor von Maltzahn 2015*
Black Sun Bk1 Excerpt – *2011 THE BLACK SUN ASCENDANT: An Assassin's Tale: Book One of the "Black Sun Series", Print Edition, copyright January 2011, ISBN 978-0-9867933-0-1*
Black Sun Bk2 Excerpt – *2015 AN EARTH ECLIPSED: An Assassin's Revenge: Book Two of the "Black Sun Series", Print Edition, copyright March 2015, ISBN 978-0-9867933-3-2*
Jasmine's Interview *Interview with Jasmine Sawant: Abridged interview, copyright March 2015*

6. **Ian**
Ian's Story *Copyright © G. Ian Stout 2015*
Dead Dog Van *Copyright © G. Ian Stout 2015*

7. **Jasmine**
Jasmine's Story *Copyright © Jasmine Sawant 2015*
Saree Kahaniyan - *Copyright © Jasmine Sawant 2012*

8. **John**
John's Story *Copyright © John Henderson 2015*
Torn Pages *Copyright © John Henderson 2015*
Have you ever had a bad day? *Copyright © John Henderson 2015*
Remember to Look UP *Copyright © John Henderson 2015*
SPACE *Copyright © John Henderson 2015*
Stop *Copyright © John Henderson 2015*
Your Mind Can Take You Places *Copyright © John Henderson 2015*
Intruder *Copyright © John Henderson 2015*
Pathways *Copyright © John Henderson 2015*
Cloudy Days *Copyright © John Henderson 2015*

Listening *Copyright © John Henderson 2015*
Memories *Copyright © John Henderson 2015*
Seasons *Copyright © John Henderson 2015*

## 9. Joseph

Joseph's Story *Copyright © Joseph A. Monachino 2015*
The Torn Page *Copyright © Joseph A. Monachino 2015*
Brigid II *Copyright © Joseph A. Monachino 2015*

## 10. Kim

Kim's Story *Copyright © Kim MacMurray2015*
Prison Life *Copyright © Kim MacMurray1986*

## 11. Meena

Glimmer it was *Copyright © Meena Chopra*
A Stillness Moves *Copyright © Meena Chopra*
Unrecognizable *Copyright © Meena Chopra*
ICONOCLAST *Copyright © Meena Chopra*
Instant in Motion *Copyright © Meena Chopra*
Potency *Copyright © Meena Chopra*
Reverberations *Copyright © Meena Chopra*
Strangers *Copyright © Meena Chopra*
Tangled in Time *Copyright © Meena Chopra*
The evolution of literature and languages of ethnic descent and the changing environment *Copyright © Meena Chopra*

## 12. Marijana

Marijana's Story *Copyright @ Marijana Gmitrovic 2015*
The One *Copyright @ Marijana Gmitrovic 2015*
The Blank Page *Copyright @ Marijana Gmitrovic 2015*
The Road *Copyright @ Marijana Gmitrovic 2015*

## 13. Mark

Mark's Story *Copyright © Mark David Garden 2015*
When Nature Calls *Copyright © Mark David Garden 2015*
How to Take a Shower *Copyright © Mark David Garden 2015*
Sense and Nonsense *Copyright © Mark David Garden 2015*

### 14. Milena

Milena's Story *Copyright © Milena Munteanu 2015*
To India and Back *Copyright © Milena Munteanu 2015*
Life as it is *Copyright © Milena Munteanu 2015*
Mount Pleasant Cemetery *Copyright © Milena Munteanu 2015*

### 15. Scott

A Strange Trip *Copyright © Scott Berger 2015*

45905695R00130

Made in the USA
Charleston, SC
07 September 2015